Dr. Ruitenbeek is a distinguished psychoanalyst and teacher in sociology, and the author of **THE INDIVIDUAL AND THE CROWD** and **FREUD AND AMERICA**. He makes his home in New York City.

The
MALE MYTH

by Hendrik M. Ruitenbeek

A DELL BOOK

Published by
DELL PUBLISHING CO., INC.
750 Third Avenue
New York, N.Y. 10017
Copyright © 1967 by Hendrik M. Ruitenbeek
Dell ® TM 681510, Dell Publishing Co., Inc.

First Dell Printing—March, 1967
Printed in U.S.A.

ACKNOWLEDGMENTS

Many thanks to Richard Huett, my editor at
Dell, who waited so patiently for this book!
And to Dr. Helene Zahler, who indeed in the
editing and counseling of this manuscript
put the feminine touch on it.

HENDRIK M. RUITENBEEK

July, 1966
New York City

for RICHARD McCONCHIE
als de wind zegt: —ik zie je, —sluit
je ogen en voel hoe ik bij je ben.
In tuinen, duizelend van oneindigheid.
                        —HANS LODEIZEN

Contents

American men don't know how to make love. . . .
American men step into marriage without the
least experience for so complicated a business.
In Europe, things are different; men take
the lead and that is as it should be.
  —SIGMUND FREUD
    in *Fragments of an Analysis with Freud,*
    by Joseph Wortis

The Male Myth

The King was saying, "I assure you, my dear,
I turned cold to the very ends of my whiskers!"
To which the Queen replied, "You haven't
got any whiskers."

—LEWIS CARROLL
from *Through the Looking-Glass*

CHAPTER I

The American Man
Analyzed

During the last decade, American journalists, psychologists, sociologists, and other observers of the social scene have given much attention to the American woman.[1] Market researchers want to know how to make her buy because she spends so much of the family income. Purveyors of cultural merchandise seek to appeal to her tastes because those tend to become the tastes of the society. Educators and politicians bid for her support because women staff the schools and possess, if they do not proportionately use, the vote. The American woman has been applauded for beauty and chic, depicted as sex symbol, denounced as mother, called destructive as wife and unsatisfying as lover. She devours and dominates, say some commenters. Others say she is overworked and underrewarded, victim of the demands of a social order which requires her to be knowledgeable parent, decorative chatelaine, impeccable housewife, and socially conscious citizen—all generally unaided by other hands than her own, however many gadgets she buys, baby-sitters she pays, or husbands she wraps in aprons and sets to tend the dishwasher. The American woman, these observers contend, is suffering from frustration of her human aspirations: her education, often superior, is wasted, her talents run to seed in the isolated routine of a suburban housewife's existence. Contrariwise, it is asserted that women's de-

mands and the competitive posture have sapped
American men. American women, it is argued, have
reduced men to creatures who no longer know who
they are and who lack confidence in themselves and
who fail to come across as self-asserting and decisive
persons.[2]

Thus, obliquely, through discussion of the position
and plight of the contemporary American woman,
some writers among those we may label as "authorized
public worriers" are studying and talking about the
American man and his problems in contemporary
society. The discussion is less in volume than that
which is devoted to the American woman, but it is
no more cheerful. American men are said to feel
threatened; they doubt themselves as males. This
doubt, it is claimed, is at least partially responsible
for the apparently purposeless violence of many
juvenile delinquents, and for the sense of loneliness
and loss which affects many other young men who live
in the community without violating its legal norms.
Doubt of their maleness affects older men, too, of
course, and in my opinion men in this age group experience the social and psychological pressures upon
their integrity as males in an even more serious degree
than younger men do. Men in their forties[3] and fifties
have often achieved sufficient economic success to be
aware that prosperity is not enough. They may have
put themselves beyond fear of material want, only
to discover that emotional and sexual security still
eludes them. Work generates emotional as well as
physical tension, for successful men in middle age
feel the sharp and subtle knives of younger competitors at their backs. Society offers little support since
the American way of life accents youth. The family
is no real refuge: American children are not accustomed to defer to their fathers and wives are often
seen, if not as competitors, at least as challenging observers. All his life, the American man lives by the

slogan, "Make good." When he reaches his late forties, many a man feels that he has not fulfilled the commandment. He experiences loneliness. He senses that even in his family he is valued less as a person than as a source of supply, material or sexual. Demands on his body and mind do not diminish as his social and economic position improves, but his confidence in his capacity to meet those demands may tend to decline. Quite contrary to the old song, the middle-aged man may feel that, whereas society allows his wife, as the mother of grown children, to rest in knowledge of labor completed, his own work can never be called done, although he runs the risk of being labeled "finished."

The Male in Peril

The average man may not yet be aware that he is in crisis. He believes that as a male his position—social, economic, and sexual—makes him superior to the female. Nevertheless, all through American society, the male's behavior shows that he actually is experiencing a change which affects his traditional roles as father, lover, and provider. This change may be summed up in a single word: emasculation. The American male is being operated on by a force other than the castrating female, however; he is being shaped by a technologically oriented culture.

Where have all the fathers gone, for example? Robert Odenwald [4] cites a five-year-old girl who said that

mothers smoke but that daddies do not, that daddies pay the bills in restaurants but that mothers give them the money beforehand; that daddies are always "nice" and that mothers are the ones who spank children when they are bad; that when the family is going some place, it is mothers who decide where to go and who make

sure that daddies and children are ready in
time; and that whenever there is trouble between
Mommy and Daddy, Mommy always tells Daddy
how bad he is.

Few people, even among social scientists and social
critics, realize the fundamental changes to which the
father has been subjected. Even the lay observer recognizes changes in the role of women and mothers;
he rather balks at the notion that the father too has
changed his social role. Too many still picture the
American father in the nineteenth-century image.
Although they may admit that the father can no longer
retain even an imitation of the authoritarian role,
they still refuse to see the father as he is in our changing society.

Has American society similarly undermined the
male as lover? The emphasis on the mechanical
aspects of our contemporary civilization has certainly
contributed to the male's increasingly mechanistic attitudes toward sexuality and the role of sex in his
life. It is less that the male cannot perform sexually
than that, too often, the sexual encounter lacks feeling
and emotion. The male complies with the sheer demands of his sexual tension, but he gains little sense
that sexuality is a positive element of his life experience, or that love is associated with sexuality. That
the mechanical aspects of our civilization affect us
(and will continue to affect us) is vividly shown in
Marshall McLuhan's rather frightening book *Understanding Media:* "Those involved in automation [he
writes] insist that it is a way of thinking, as much
as it is a way of doing." [5] One cannot help but wonder
whether the shift in the position of the American male
as father represents emasculation by the technological
elements in our society. One wonders, too, whether his
emasculation merely reflects our trend from a human-
directed culture toward a culture directed not to hu-

man beings but to the mechanical and electronic environment they have made for themselves.

If the role of the male as lover has changed—in some measure because women can make much more forthright sexual demands upon their men—his role as provider has altered almost as drastically. Once again, the partner who had to take what was offered now has an increasing range of choice. Traditionally, the role of provider has made the father the source of life for the family, not merely the person who furnished a livelihood for the household. I remember vividly how, during my own childhood, loss of the father meant the breakup of the family unless relatives stepped in to supply the money needed to keep mother and children together. Such situations are exceptional in contemporary America. Women are quite capable of earning a living for themselves and their children. The male thus is no longer indispensable for family survival. However important his presence may be psychologically, economically he is no longer necessary. What was once an exceptional situation—the woman-supported household—is now quite commonplace, and not merely among the very poor.

Quite frequently nowadays, wives work while their husbands carry on their studies. This situation is not entirely unprecedented, to be sure. Women—particularly among certain immigrant groups—have often worked to support fiancés studying to become doctors and the like. But such couples usually did not marry until the man could be an effective breadwinner. The deprivations of a long (and presumably chaste) engagement seemed easier to bear than depletion of the man's traditional role as provider. Young people are no longer willing to accept such deprivation. As St. Paul counseled, they marry rather than burn. The woman who earns the family living at the outset of the marriage no longer sees her husband as provider. And he, living on what she earns, often finds it diffi-

cult to see himself as breadwinner. Children come
early to these marriages, but often wives return to
work and continue to share the economic burden of
the family. Children no longer grow up taking for
granted that it is their fathers who supply their needs.
And though young men accept their wives' necessary
help, they often feel somewhat emasculated by the
loss of control which the wife as wage earner may
represent.

The situation just sketched is most common among
young men who marry while they are in graduate
school. Yet the working wife is taken for granted in
older middle-class households. The expense of living
as well as suburban neighbors do, the cost of children's education, the feeling among many college
women that they are wasted as housewives, awareness
that they may need to earn money when they are
widowed—all of these factors send middle-class women
into the labor market. Once again, the male feels his
masculinity eroded by this deprivation of his traditional role as provider.

The Revolt of Women

Much of the material referred to in the foregoing
discussion implies that in their relationship with
American women, American men have somehow suf-
fered defeat. That in turn has made them feel insecure, socially and sexually; hence the male in the
United States is in a precarious condition and one
that is likely to become more precarious as time goes
on. Once, the superiority of men was taken for
granted, by themselves and by everyone else. Now
that superiority is felt to be challenged. Gone is the
image of the strong father, the domineering or dominating husband, the wise grandsire, the manly son.

In the household and outside, the contemporary
American man seems threatened by the assertive and

aggressive woman, and this, oddly enough, in the post-Freudian age, when women have learned that they are supposed to be passive, receptive, supportive, and loving. Popular culture—the world of the comic strip, the radio and TV serial, although interestingly enough, not the confession magazine—may say father knows best, but it frequently portrays him as hood-winked by brash children and governed by a sweetly wise wife.

Men may have felt exploited by their children before, and the woman who twists men around her little finger is a stereotype. What is novel in the contemporary situation—particularly in the United States—is what seems like an approach to a reversal of sexual roles, or at least a dilution of them, as women become more active and men more passive.

Western civilization is based on the belief that the family is the cornerstone of society and that men dominate the family. Perhaps, Weston LaBarre says, human culture began when father came home to stay—that is, when the male developed the pattern of remaining with the female, helping her feed and rear their offspring. Perhaps, too, women did invent agriculture and so make settled life possible. But weaponry and the taming of useful beasts seem to have been male contributions, along with war and the political state. Thereafter, men fought, thought, and taught. They owned the land and decided how it was to be tilled. They provided the food; they decided who was to share it. They gave orders; they governed; they made the decisions. Women were necessary and present, but they were expected to remain in the background—unless they were queens or princesses, and even then their position was generally that of their royal fathers or husbands (although remnants of an-other situation can, indeed, be found in history). Heir-esses often were disposed of like other property. Wom-en were the spoils of war, not its makers. They wor-

shipped the gods; they did not invent theologies. They
obeyed the law—or evaded it; they did not establish
it. Women had the power to turn a man's life sour,
but only in private; in public, women (when they
were allowed to be visible) were to be seen, not
heard.

Folklore and fiction show men distrusting women,
successfully deceived by women, even murdered by
women, but Bluebeard killed seven wives before
Fatima outwitted him—and she survived only because
her brothers came to help her. Helen of Troy was at
least half a goddess. And Clytemnestra paid for her
crime. All of these heroines—Clytemnestra herself ex-
cepted, perhaps—were passive, responding to men,
not initiating action on their own.

Again, men may have suspected that their women
were mocking them. Men must have feared impotence,
or they would not have invented stories like the
Apocrypha's tale of the woman possessed of a devil
who made it impossible for her husband to consum-
mate marriage. But if men doubted their sexual effi-
ciency, they tended to keep those doubts to themselves. They experienced sexual difficulties, but they
did not feel those difficulties as symptoms of a breakdown in the relationship between themselves, their
women, and their society. In ancient times, the Western world apparently considered homosexuality as a
diversion—vulgar or elegant as the temper of the culture or the person might dictate—or a phase of human
development; it was part of the mores rather than
evidence of a fissure within them.

The literature of the Middle Ages, to move on from
the reaches of antiquity, provides plenty of evidence
about sexual deviations, failures, and excesses. The
Knights Templar, to cite one instance, were accused
of all sorts of sexual perversions. Witches not only
had intercourse with the devil, but were charged with
making men impotent. If blasphemy and religious

rebellion were sometimes orgiastic, heresy, like that of the Albigensians, might carry sexual excess to the opposite pole and deny the flesh altogether, not merely to a chosen few—professed monks, nuns, and priests—but to all who hoped for salvation.

All this, however, was mere individual experience; it did not enter into the male's picture of himself because no real change occurred in the position of women. They enjoyed no greater share in the medieval state than they had in antiquity. They had no greater ability to dispose of themselves or determine the course of their lives. They had no greater control of property.

In politics, in the arts, in religion, in philosophy, men's influence has been dominant for thousands of years. Power, learning, creativity—barring a few noteworthy exceptions—have been male prerogatives. Men have made the laws, the wars, and the epics. They have painted the pictures, hewn the statues, constructed the universes of discourse; they have invented the machines, manipulated the markets, piled up and played with the millions. Male domination has been the rule for so long that each claim of women, as it was made, seemed like a separate and intolerable blasphemy. Ironically, it was men's actions in altering the economy which changed society in ways that made almost inevitable the movement which we may label the "revolt of women." The Industrial Revolution destroyed first the stable, or at least the slow-moving, agricultural society and then the economically functioning home which had been necessary to that society. Step by step, the work which had been woman's was taken from her: either it was now done by men, or women had to leave home to do it. They were paid for what they did with money and, ultimately, they became responsible for their own livelihoods. In most Western countries, women achieved a greater or lesser degree of social emancipation: they asserted a new and more directly felt influence in all the areas of human activity and, consequently, in the orbit of male concern.

At this point, we confront one of the most interesting aspects of the situation of the male in contemporary America, where modern social trends have their most unimpeded impact. An old American slang phrase runs: when you're at the top, you've no place to go but down. In respect to the relationship between men and women, insofar as that relation involves domination and subordination, change had to undermine men's authority and the security of their traditional position. Men were in command; shifts would weaken that command.

The Roots of Peril

Because of the peculiar historical experience of the United States, the new position of women is especially evident here, and this even though women as politicians and professional persons are rather more conspicuous in England and France, for example, than they are in this country. European men appear to retain more of their old position than the Americans. Is it perhaps that American men do not yet enjoy the scarcity value which two world wars have given males in Europe? Whatever the reason, the altered situation of the male seems most visible in the United States. That altered situation, I would emphasize, is no mere response to the emancipation of women. The aggressive female, especially in the shape of the castrating oedipal mother, has become an all too easy target; to make her responsible for the weaknesses and deficiencies of the American man is only to push the question one step backward: how is it, we may ask, that the American woman, sturdy pioneer that she may have been, could have been able to exert so diminishing an effect on the American man—who was as much

a pioneer as she? Rather, the changed position of
men and women alike is to be attributed to the rapid
and continuous change which has long characterized
American society.

Early in the nineteenth century, for example, Alexis
de Tocqueville wrote:

> In the United States a man builds a house in
> which to spend his old age, and he sells it before
> the roof is on; he plants a garden and lets it go
> just as the trees are coming into bearing; he
> brings a field into tillage and leaves other men to
> gather the crops; he embraces a profession and
> gives it up; he settles in a place which he soon
> afterwards leaves to carry his changeable long-
> ings elsewhere. If his private affairs leave him
> any leisure, he instantly plunges into the vortex
> of politics; and if at the end of a year of un-
> remitting labor he finds he has a few days' va-
> cation, his eager curiosity whirls him over the
> vast extent of the United States, and he will travel
> fifteen hundred miles in a few days to shake off
> his happiness. Death at length overtakes him, but
> it is before he is weary of his bootless chase of
> that complete felicity which forever escapes him.[°]

Instability and restlessness have long been norms of
American behavior, then. Without those qualities,
Americans would never have forced settlement across
the stubborn breadth of a continent in a mere two
centuries, reckoning from the settlement of Jamestown
to the decade before World War I. Mobility was a
mark of maleness in early America. Lumberman, fish-
erman, trapper, hunter, Indian fighter, boatman,
miner, cowboy—all the heroic shapes of American
legend are men who work and move on, men without
women, males with neither home nor family, who buy
women, when the commodity is available, and expend

their emotions—when they permit themselves to experience emotions—on each other.

The pioneer farmer and his family were themselves
almost as mobile as any trapper of them all. Before
railroads were built, a move of fifty miles west would
usually carry a family from settled country into what
was almost wilderness, and there, however useful
women might be, men ruled; they subdued the land—
and they decided when they wanted new land to sub-
due. Their women had to move with them—unless they
preferred the cold maintenance of the local poorhouse
or the bitter support of some reluctant male relative.

There was little stability, social or physical, when
all the American world seemed ready to pack up and
move on. Yet despite the instability experienced by
the movers, they were not deprived of a sense of self-
determination. They knew what they wanted to do.
They felt that they could do what they wanted. Their
knowledge helped them establish that sense of who
and what they were—and who and what they were
not—the sense of *identity*.

Establishing Male Identity

The conditions of life in pre-industrial America all
but required that the male establish his identity in
terms of aggressive, self-determining individuation.
The introduction of machine industry hampered but
did not destroy old paths toward achieving male identity. Insofar as industrialism offered new opportunities
for economic mobility, men in America found ample
room for achieving their identity in traditional terms:
a man was a person who took an active, aggressive
stance vis-à-vis society and, particularly, vis-à-vis
women. Women were subordinate; by definition, men
were their rulers. However little a man might be able
to rule his situation in store, mine, or factory, in his
own home—if he had a home—he was the master. Yet,

this may have been less true than it was in industrialized Europe, for we hear about the rebellious American child and the demanding American wife in the nineteenth century, too.

Pressures have increased since then and the increase has been cumulative both in quantity and in speed. Less and less can the average man feel himself in full control of his existence; more and more people, as Peter Blau says, earn their livings as employees and moreover as employees of large organizations. Too often, those employees are not valued in proportion to skill and initiative but in proportion to their ability to get along with other people and work as one of a team. The distinctively masculine characteristics of activity and overt aggressiveness seem to be becoming less useful than the traditionally feminine characteristics of manipulative beguilement or conciliation of other people. Thus, it becomes more difficult to establish a distinctively masculine identity in other than purely sexual terms. One cannot help asking whether sexuality itself can bear so large a burden. As we shall see, sexual maleness seems often to be depleted among men who find it difficult to establish themselves as males in other, more social terms.

The problem of establishing any kind of identity in so fluid a society as that of contemporary America, for all that one may see signs of a hardening of classes, is further intensified by the broadening of the world with which people come into contact. During most of human history, only a few people have moved any distance from the places of their birth; their contact with strangers has been limited. Now this has all changed; an increasing number of people are exposed to contact with more and more distant places and events. More and more people know that what happens far away can affect their lives. Again, this has been true for many generations, particularly in the United

States; the novel element in the situation is the greater awareness of it by growing numbers of people.

Erik Erikson tells how changes in the contemporary world differ both in kind and in degree from those which men have experienced before:

> The ubiquity of nuclear threat, the break-through into outer space, and increasing global communication are all bringing about a total change in the sense of geographic space and of historical time and thus necessitate a redefinition of the identity of the sexes within a new image of man.[7]

This nuclear age challenges male leadership in a peculiar way. As governors and as military leaders, men have had it within their power to destroy cities, nations, even whole cultures, but they have never had it within their power to destroy the human race. And this power seems the end of all their mastery.

Erikson contends, with much cogency, that the male identity is rooted in men's identification with "what works," whether that be the penis or the polity. Today, it has become necessary for men to face the need to subordinate "what works"—that is, technological and politico-military achievement—to the sheer preservation of the human species. But preservation, care for the continuity of life, is the traditional portion of women, who have the role of nurturing the children who are the visible human future. The care of children is work, of course, and sometimes very laborious work, but only lately, reckoned according to the long span of history, has the care of children become something other than a traditional, almost an instinctive activity. Men have found their identity in their work rather than in an extension of their biological function (however much, from the psychoanalytic viewpoint, men's work may be a series of transformations of that biological activity). Identification as some variety of worker and the achievement of identity through work have been especially important to the American man, for here his primary function has been carrying on some kind of business, whether in agriculture, industry, trade, or finance. As I have noted earlier in this chapter, the American man was able to involve himself in his work sufficiently to derive from it both a sense of identity and a feeling of stability in that identity. He could communicate his confidence in himself as man and father and so offer a model for his sons to follow and his daughters to recognize.

As work has become mechanized, as control of opportunity to work has passed out of the individual's power in many instances, and as routine work is itself more occupied with relating to people and less with producing goods, many men have lost the sense that excitement and discovery are associated with the way they earn their living. Even lifting a burden may be linked with feelings of achievement and strength as it gives the laborer a chance to show how powerful a body he has; similarly, a man may feel the potent male when he operates a fork-lift truck dexterously. Yet, as time-and-motion study is applied and perfected and as men are increasingly told *how* to do their daily tasks, those tasks leave decreasing room for men to feel that their work offers scope and support for the sense of being male. Few people can enjoy the awareness of creativity which comes to the artist or the scientist at the moment of discovery, but most men need to feel that their daily lives make some demands on, and offer some support for, aggressiveness and activity.

The Depletion of Work

For American men who earn their living in business, particularly in business which is not directly concerned

with the production of *goods, status* has become a
prime objective, a way to show that one is a man.
Status and economic reward go together, as a rule;
the American man still wants to make money, but he
does not often hope to become a captain of industry
in the nineteenth-century style. His desire for economic
achievement does not seem animated by the kind of
passion his grandfather may have shown; passion itself often seems outside his emotional range. He
wants the kind of recognition which Edward Ziegler
describes:

> At another New York City corporation that is
> housed in a more modest 30-story building, there
> is such an obvious hierarchy of departments by
> floor that some members of middle management
> talk of the "gamma-15 effect," which is their
> way of describing the distinct drop-off in status
> of people below the fifteenth floor. According to
> their scheme, people are ranked according to
> the *Brave New World* system: alpha being a su-
> perior status holder, beta, above-average; gam-
> ma, average; delta, below-average; and epsilon,
> abysmally low in status. You can tell the differ-
> ence, they claim, simply by listening to the
> amount of noise on each floor. "Deltas make about
> three times more noise than betas," they explain.[8]

David Riesman gives us other insights into the relationship between the contemporary position of the
American male and that which he enjoyed in an older
world where both the social context and the values it
generated gave at least a measure of support to the
male identity:

> The economy was quite loose-jointed and im-
> personal and perhaps seemed even more imper-
> sonal than it actually was. This encouraged the

ambitious labors of men who could attend to society's expanding capital plant, to the bottle-necks in the technology of agriculture, extractive industry, and manufacturing. The capital goods industries were of decisive importance; internally, they were needed to bridge the gap between pop-ulation and subsistence; externally, they were needed to support war-making and colonization. Indeed, the oversteered men of the period, espe-cially in the regions touched by Puritanism and Jansenism, went far beyond the specifically eco-nomic requirements and rewards held out to them. They cut themselves off from family and friends, often from humanity in general, by their assiduity and diligence.

Work, one might add, provided a strategic protection for those who could not live up to all the requirements of the prevailing character ideal. For we have no right to assume that even the successful men of the period were in complete adjustment with the social character imposed on them. Many apparently well-adjusted men of an older time in American life must have been aware that their acceptance of inner-direction involved their own efforts to conform—that their conformity was far from automatic.[9]

In other words, work meant choosing activity over inactivity and both choice and the activity growing out of it allowed American man to regard himself as a male. Blau and Ziegler show how economic change has operated to create a new relationship between men and their work. This new relationship offers less than the old in the way of direct gratifica-tion of one's needs as a male. Aggressiveness, power, the capacity to dominate—these are still demanded of men, for these characteristics mark the model of what a male should be. But contemporary society has little room for the forthright expression of these characteristics in socially acceptable ways (except in war). Psychoanalytically speaking, castrating forces have multiplied and directly potentiating forces have diminished. Only juvenile delinquents kill with their own hands; we expect to fight the next war long distance. "Gentlemen's agreements" not only fix prices in some sectors of contemporary industry; they prevail in other ways and so allow smaller enterprises to exist alongside large corporations which could destroy them. The "smiler with the knife" may be at work in the upper echelons of management, but his smile may be as important as his knife. The skillful user of people is more likely to succeed than the ruthless subduer of them.

Sex and Masculinity

In one sense, we may say that American life has been feminized. In a castrating environment, men feel their women to be another castrating influence, a constant and debilitating challenge to the potency, the sexuality which may well seem the last fortress of masculinity. Sociologists have much to say about an increasing rate of male homosexuality. Psychoanalysts, too, are concerned with this, but they are also aware of a high level of sheer sexual impotence among their patients. It seems likely that many men marry in order to convince society—and themselves—that they are adequately male. For in our Western culture, maleness is only partially demonstrated by sexual activity outside of marriage. To be sure, the marriage bond is less of a shackle than it was in our grandfathers' time. Divorce is common, infidelity more common still. Premarital chastity is no longer generally demanded of a middle-class bride; the middle-class wife is allowed to stray. Yet this freedom merely adds another dimension to the problem that the American man encounters in establishing a gratifying, or indeed any, male identity. Before World War I, unmarried men were apt to turn to socially inferior women for sex, and wives, by convention, were supposed to be satisfied with the kinds of sexual experience their husbands provided. Now, the middle-class American, to use a psychoanalytic metaphor, must face his mother in almost every woman's bed he enters; even the "call girl" may be of his own social class. Thus, in a society which gives him minimal support in establishing himself as a male, the American man must meet a peculiarly intense challenge to prove himself sexually effective. So sharp is the challenge that undercurrents of protests are becoming visible; a writer like Leslie Farber in his recent book *The Ways of the Will* [10] can at least imply that since many women never experience true sexual orgasm, and since they did not expect to do so in other times, contemporary women should not expect to reach climax, and, particularly, they should not make men feel inadequate if they do not meet their sexual partner's demands.

The American man is said to feel threatened in a way that goes far beyond the insecurity generated by living in a constantly changing economy and a political world where rulers who do not seem unusually notable for goodness or wisdom have the means with which to end civilization as we know it—if not to make man an extinct species. The American man, young as well as aging, is said to feel that his very maleness is in peril; that he is being emasculated. Many factors are said to contribute to his lack of confidence, notably the disintegration of the patriarchal family and the emancipation of the women who live in it. I should like to suggest a change of emphasis: in a mobile society where the economy is moving rapidly and in a direction which seems to give less scope for the forthright exercise of the activity and aggressiveness we

think of as male, sexuality seems to be the one area
in which the male is protected from the impact of
technological change: automation may replace even
management with machines, but it does not seem
likely to make the penis obsolete.

One can say that sexuality is apparently becoming
the chief attribute of maleness, but sexuality itself
seems threatened. The Kinsey report and the flood
of discussion about the American man's sexuality indicate a broad questioning of his ability to fill his sexual
role. The American man seems oddly ready to evaluate
himself in terms of his sexual performance. The Kinsey
report—however justified criticism of its method may
be—indicates how varied that performance may be.
Yet many American men are willing to measure their
worth in terms of books like the *Sexually Adjusted
Male*. Such overemphasis on one phase of sexuality,
incidentally, is paralleled by other sorts of overemphasis in discussions of the problems of the male
in America. So we have the cluster of emphases which
might be labeled "It's all women's fault," for they are
competitive and demanding instead of passive and
comforting. As a result, men have become impotent,
promiscuous, afraid of homosexuality, afraid to remain
unmarried past the age of thirty, unable to present a
stable masculine image for their children to use as
model. Other sociologists stress the breakdown of
traditional family patterns and sociosexual roles in a
society which changes so fast that old values are
destroyed before their irrelevance is noticed and new
values become obsolescent before they can take effective hold of the emotions.

In my opinion, the American man's difficulty in resisting the forces making for emasculation go far
beyond mere distortions or disturbances in sexual
functioning or sexual expectation. Rather, he (like the
American woman) is experiencing alienation from
himself and from his society; he is suffering from the

failure of identity which accompanies such alienation. Alienation has many aspects, and I shall discuss some of them in later chapters. The crisis in identity too has many facets, and I shall deal with a number of those. Hopefully, this approach to the problem will allow us to draw upon a variety of insights—sexual, psychological, and sociological—while avoiding overemphasis on any one. In this way, our exploration of the situation of the male in contemporary America may help broaden our understanding of several current socio-psychological problems.

Men talk or fight;
they do not grease machines
or even draw blueprints.
—DAVID RIESMAN
in *Individualism Reconsidered*

CHAPTER II

The American Man
and Society

If we are to understand the contemporary position and problems of the American male, we must pay some attention to the relationship between maleness and society. We must also glance backward to see the position from which the American male has moved—or been pushed—since the nineteenth century. Only then can we profitably approach such issues as the absorption of maleness into the social framework and the possible decline of masculine influence in the United States today.

The Genesis of Maleness

Psychoanalytic theory maintains that the boy establishes his awareness of himself as a male person in the course of his resolution of the oedipal conflict. The male infant (here resembling the female) first feels himself to be part of his mother. Then, differentiating himself from her, he desires his mother as the source of all good things, of life itself. His desire soon acquires a more clearly sexual coloring and he comes to know his father as rival. The rival is successful. The boy hates his father-rival, yet he admires and loves him. Admiration may be a method for transforming envy of the superior strength and sexual capability which give the father possession of the mother. Love, too, may be a transformation of the boy's fear and guilt, fear lest he be punished for aggressive wishes against the father, guilt at having such wishes.

39

Out of this mingling of emotion grows the small boy's desire to resemble his rival. The boy, to put it otherwise, "identifies" with his father and, through that identification, all confused though it may be, he comes to know himself as a male.

Sexual Revolution

What it means to be a male depends very materially upon the society in which the boy grows up. Every normal male infant is born with the appropriate glandular and anatomical equipment; every normal male infant also experiences some form of the basic oedipal conflict. What he does with his fundamental experience and basic biological structure is another matter.

All societies, as Margaret Mead points out, differentiate the male role from the female. All societies, too, change and so alter their expectations of what those roles should be. If we survey the social record, we see that the behavior considered proper for the sex roles may differ widely from one culture or society to the next. More important for our inquiry, the character of a given society may make it either easy or difficult for a boy to look upon himself as a male and to exhibit the behavior appropriate to the male role. A relatively stable society dominated by men gives psychological support to the growing male; a rapidly changing society where women, uncertain of their own identity and role, assert personal independence may appear to deny psychological support to maleness or even to threaten its existence and development.

A psychologist who looks back at England or the United States in the nineteenth century might speculate that a society which dampened the sexuality of respectable women would tend to support masculinity since it would operate to lesson the pressure for sexual performance. Fromm observes that, whereas women need only accept, men must function sexually;

men run the risk of failure and consequent loss of self-esteem. Folklore and custom alike bear witness to men's belief that women are sexually demanding—and therefore threatening as well as delightful. A situation which diminishes the demand may well be especially reassuring to the male.

And such a situation did apparently develop during the past century.[1] Human energy is limited, or so it may be argued. If energy and attention are focused on sex, they are diverted from other activities, notably the individual male's economic advancement. Gandhi, for example, deplored the Indian custom of early marriage because it turned young men from their books to their brides. Montaigne, too, urged men to marry soberly and not expend an unbecoming passion on their wives. If sex is reduced to routine, in marriage or outside, then men are freed for other activities. We may interpret certain nineteenth-century British and American sexual attitudes accordingly. During a period of maturing and expanding industrialism middle-class men, particularly, needed to regard success in business as their prime reason for existence. They could spare little time for elaborating sexual behavior. In one respect at least, the nineteenth-century middle-class male was in an enviable position: no woman had any right to question his sexual adequacy. His wife was not supposed to have any sexual needs. She was pure, by definition, and consequently merely yielded to her husband's animal nature; she did not wish to participate in his "low pleasure." Other men's wives and unmarried women of one's own class were pure, too, and not to be trifled with. Prostitutes, available in more than sufficient numbers, could make no claim. Consequently, a man could regard himself as adequate sexually whatever the character of his performance.

But this Eden proved impermanent. Industrial society finally offered some ladies (as well as great num-

bers of lower-class women) employment and incomes
that did not depend on men. More and more middle-
class women began to assert a claim to higher-paying
work with a greater degree of status. Women demanded access to education. They secured the right
to vote. They claimed the right to pleasures once reserved to men. They began to clamor for an end to the
"double standard" which required girls to be chaste
but allowed youths to be dissolute (provided that they
restricted dissipation to "fair game" areas—lower class
girls or prostitutes). And finally, women asserted their
right to sexual satisfaction in marriage. Before World
War I, and as late as the 1930's perhaps, wives might
claim emotional understanding and appreciation from
their husbands, but they were not often supposed to
question what they received sexually. Now, even conventional women expect sexual satisfaction and will
be quite ready to engage in frank discussion of any
perceived inadequacy in husband or boyfriend. Such
attitudes—and men's awareness that the women with
whom they may become intimate are willing to sit in
sexual judgment on them—may in effect be castrating.

Women's increasing effort to accept themselves
as sexual beings entitled to sexual satisfaction constitutes something approaching a revolution. That
revolution, if a turning away from nineteenth-century
mores may be called a revolution, has come at a
specially hazardous moment for the American male
since it removes, or at least undermines, a significant
prop to maleness at the very time when the society
itself is experiencing change at a rate and of a quality
which further threatens men's confidence in their
masculinity.

Character Types and Masculinity

If we use David Riesman's convenient formulation,
society has shifted from a producing, inner-directed

basis to a consuming, other-directed basis. From the economic point of view, our society is concerned not with activities which Colin Clark would label "primary"—agriculture and manufacturing—but with trade and finance—the exchange and marketing of goods and services. It has become easier for the economy to make things than to sell them. The goods made, moreover, are often "necessary" by social convention rather than by utility: a contemporary automobile is marketed as a status symbol rather than as a means of transportation; a good deal of contemporary entertainment, even, is pursued as much for display as for enjoyment. Increasingly, the successful man is one who can manipulate people rather than one who can deal efficiently with things.

Traditionally, however, in our society the small-scale manipulation of people has been women's work; a man is supposed to achieve his purpose directly, by objective means, rather than by persuading other people that his purposes are theirs. In contemporary America—and to somewhat lesser degree in contemporary industrialized Atlantic Europe—men's work requires an approach which increasingly resembles the wiles once considered appropriate to women. Our society has long looked upon the distinctively feminine with ambivalent regard; "womanish" is no complimentary word; "feminine" is often equated with "inferior." Hence when men are required to behave in ways conventionally considered characteristic of women, their confidence and masculinity tend to be shaken. And for a male reared in our tradition diminished masculinity means lessened worth.

If we turn from the economy to the society in which that economy operates, we can see how the shift from concentration on the production and control of basic needs—food, transportation, and the like—to the marketing of goods which are often of only imagined utility—one brand of detergent rather than another, say—has produced the change in character which David Riesman describes as the movement from the inner-directed to the other-directed man.

In old-fashioned societies where men earn their living by working the land (or by taxing those who do the work), people are guided by tradition. The best man, morally and socially, is he who does as his father did. Acting according to custom is good, innovating is, on the whole, bad.

Such a society may be psychologically comfortable and even artistically creative but it does not develop the capacity to spew forth a continuously increasing quantity of goods. If European society was to become productive in the contemporary sense, men would have to change, to make thrift, prudence, and the pursuit of wealth their guides. Not doing as one's father had, but the energetic pursuit of wealth was to become the characteristic quality of "essential human nature."

In England, and then in the United States, a distinct type of character won prime esteem. This inner-directed man, to use Riesman's term, so completely accepts the dictate of a particular phase of social development that he makes them part of himself. Thus the inner-directed person feels that he acts from within. He does not rely upon custom and tradition. He does not generally admit he looks to his contemporaries for guidance although one must recognize that the nineteenth-century England and America which Riesman uses to show a high level of inner-direction also were notorious for obedience to "Mrs. Grundy," that is, to social pressure. Mrs. Grundy was visualized, incidentally, as a middle-aged, middle-class woman distinguished by a singularly dirty-minded prudery and noteworthy for censorious hostility to every kind of enjoyment, particularly among the lower classes. Not consumption but attention to business was the proper end of man.

The inner-directed character was well suited to develop men who lived to accumulate capital so that they could produce more goods at a profit which would let them accumulate more capital so that they could produce more goods—until the channels of trade choked with them. If the choked channels were to be cleared effectively, a new character type had to emerge. Not thrift and prudence but the desire to have and to show now became useful. The economy needed a high level of consumption to keep going. The inner-directed producing man had to recede before the other-directed consuming man.

The other-directed man is aware (as the inner-directed person is not) that his behavior and his emotional responses do not come entirely from within anymore. The other-directed man admits that he looks to his contemporaries for direction. Instead of looking within and listening for the "still small voice," he looks around and listens to "the commercials," the "in" people or his psychotherapist!

If we accept the convention that a man should act independently, according to his own reasoned convictions, whereas a woman should act as directed by father, husband, and respectable society, we may say that contemporary other-directed character clashes with the common definition of masculinity. Other-direction seems far more consonant with what is regarded as a properly feminine approach to life.

Another observer of contemporary society, Allen Wheelis put it thus in his *The Quest for Identity:*

> The change in social character is often described as a decline of individualism; but individualism means many things, and not all of them have declined. Individualism means self-reliance, productive self-sufficiency, following one's chosen course despite social criticism, and bearing personally the risk of one's undertakings; and all of

these are on the wane. Ours is an age of reliance
on experts, of specialized production, of deference
to public opinion, and of collective security. But
individualism means, also, the awareness of individuality, and this has increased. For accompanying the other changes there has occurred an
extension of awareness.[2]

  Here, too, we can see a shift of emphasis from what
is generally regarded as a masculine attitude. Women
are supposed to defer to public opinion, to depend on
others for security, to rely on the judgment of people
better trained than themselves. But sensitivity and
awareness have long been considered a feminine preserve; women were supposed to be intuitive, knowing
what others wanted and eager to meet their needs.

Inner-Direction as Support

What was the position of the male in the inner-
directed society? He did face challenge, for he func-
tioned in a competitive world, but that challenge
came from other men. All the rewarding occupations
belonged to men. Women had no place in the professions. If they did own business enterprises, those were
small. Working women generally were confined to
monotonous, low-paying jobs. If a woman did earn
large sums—as dancer, actress, or expensive prostitute
—it was usually by serving male needs; certainly her
success rarely if ever made her a competitor of men
however skillfully and profitably she might exploit
them.

In the family, men enjoyed an assured position.
Wives served and pampered their husbands; if they
did not, they were criticized. They had very limited
legal rights over earnings or property, if they had
either; their children belonged to their husbands (at
least under English law); they could be divorced for

adultery, but they could not exact fidelity from their husbands; even separate maintenance was difficult to secure. Whatever they might feel, they did not express dissatisfaction with being housewives; they claimed no right to fulfilment as persons on the sexual or any other level. Sisters took second place to their brothers: on the Continent, their dowries might be skimped so that their brothers could cut a proper figure; or, they might be disposed of in marriage to benefit their families and with small concern for their own wishes. Servants relieved the wife of the care of the household and children. She was liberated to adorn the ballroom and salon; she might even have lovers. The American wife, on the other hand, often had to cope with inefficient servants, inadequate schools, and the social rule that married women should tend to their homes and children: they might be chaperones but their dancing days were over. Children, of course, were "to be seen and not heard" (a command not always obeyed in American households); they were expected to remain at a polite distance from the father, about whom the family revolved.

This situation is clearly portrayed in Gide's *If It Die:*

> My father was taken up preparing his lectures at the faculty of law and gave very little of his time to me. He spent most of the day shut up in a vast and rather dark study, into which I was only allowed when he expressly invited me. . . . I had a veneration for my father which was slightly mixed with fear and which was enhanced by the solemnity of this abode. I went into it as into a temple; the bookcase rose out of the gloom like a tabernacle; a thick carpet of a dark rich colour stifled the sound of my footsteps. . . . My father had very special ideas as to what should be read to me—ideas that were not shared by my mother; and I used often to hear them discuss

what was the proper nourishment for a child's mind. Similar discussions sometimes arose on the subject of obedience, my mother holding that a child should obey without trying to understand, my father always inclining to explain everything to me. . . . Sometimes on fine summer evenings, when we had not supped too late, and when my father was not too busy, he used to say: "Would my little friend like to come for a walk?" He never called me anything but his "little friend." . . . I liked going out with my father; and as he rarely gave me any of his time, the few things we did together had an unfamiliar, solemn and rather mysterious air about them which delighted me. . . . Sometimes we still had time to walk back through the big Luxembourg Gardens. But a rub-a-dub of drums soon gave notice it was closing time. The last visitors reluctantly turned towards the exits, with the park-keepers close at their heels, and behind them the broad garden walks, now left deserted, filled slowly up with mystery. On those evenings I went to bed intoxicated with darkness, sleep and strangeness.[3]

Even when children, sons particularly, were in conflict with their fathers, they did not cast aside their regard for them. Franz Kafka draws an envying portrait of the authoritative inner-directed father when he writes:

I recognize you have—just everything together, good and bad, just as it is organically united in you, viz., strength and contempt for others, health and a certain excess, eloquence and stand-offishness, self-confidence and dissatisfaction with everybody else, superiority to the world and tyranny, knowledge of the world and distrust of most people in it, and then advantages with no disadvantage attached, such as industry, endurance, presence of mind, fearlessness.[4]

Vincent van Gogh did not like his father, yet quarrels and antagonism did not break the bond, the feeling that an indissoluble relationship existed, continuing no matter what hostility might exist. He describes a visit:

Father has been here, and I was so glad he came. The most pleasant recollection of his visit is of a morning we spent together in my little room, correcting some work and talking over several things. You can imagine the days flew by, and when I had seen him off at the station, and had looked after the train as long as it was in sight, even the smoke of it, then came home to my room and saw Father's chair still standing near the little table on which the books and copy books of the day before were still lying, though I know that we shall see each other again pretty soon, I cried like a child.[5]

Undermining the Pillars

An expanding economy and a social structure which offered stimulating challenge spurred the inner-directed man to achievement, yet did not deplete his confidence in his adequacy as a male. He was thus fortunately situated, if he belonged to the upper or middle class. No well-behaved wife questioned her husband's ability as provider. In no proper family did he face inquiry into his authority as a father. His work often gave scope for his own initiative and his own thinking. Even as an employee, he could see himself as directing his working life to a far greater degree than is possible in contemporary large business enterprises with their bureaucratic lines of command depicted in elaborate organizational charts. Whatever ultimate consequences the use of computers may have for middle management, responsibility has already been eroded; in many instances, success depends on ability to claim credit for other men's work and to disclaim blame for one's own errors.

Here again, the tortuous, conventionally feminine method of handling situations, tends to replace the direct, traditionally masculine posture. A contemporary man may identify with his organization, but he can rarely conceive of his work as part of himself. In the nineteenth century, American men might move from place to place and occupation to ocupation, but they could usually feel that their mobility was the result of choice rather than economic compulsion or mere drifting with the tide. It was easier to think of oneself as necessary, as if one would really be missed.

In the contemporary world, only a singularly obtuse man is unaware of how expendable he is, how easily he can be replaced. Only genius leaves a hole when it disappears, and contemporary society seems to have less and less need for the genius it is so ready to acclaim. In business, in politics, in profession, each man knows he is dispensable. The corporation can carry on as well without him; the scientific project will proceed quite as well as if he were still on its staff; the government department will do its work although another man sits at his desk. The psychotherapist who believes a man's work to be closely related to his sexuality might well conclude that contemporary society thus attacks rather then supports men's confidence in their masculinity. Certainly, the average middle-class man knows he can be replaced as father and husband. If he should die, his wife will run the family as usual. If he is divorced, and the chances are good that he will be, his children will accept another father.

Nevertheless, American young men seem no longer

to feel comfortable as bachelors. During the nineteenth century, a middle-class young man was not
supposed to marry until he had reasonably good prospects of supporting a wife and family. Estimates of
the character of those prospects might vary, of course;
men might take on the risks and responsibilities of
marriage earlier in the United States than in England,
perhaps, but postponement bore no stigma. The young
bachelor was a customary part of social life, but the
middle-aged man who had not married and proclaimed that he had no intention of marrying was
also a familiar and quite acceptable figure. He might
be envied; he might be found fault with for being too
selfish to assume a family man's cares, but he was not
generally thought to be a psychological oddity.[6] Today in contrast, a man past thirty who has never been
married is all but immediately labeled neurotic,
"mother's boy," or homosexual.

Increasingly, social pressure pushes young people
toward early marriage. Girls have always been somewhat fearful of being left on the shelf, of course, but
now young men, too, feel pushed toward obedience to
the commandment: achieve the $12,000-a-year wage
bracket, three children, and a home in the suburbs by
twenty-five. A young man who has not reached these
goals feels himself a failure, immature, deficient as a
male. Yet marriage and a family immediately after
completing college often seem a threatening prospect,
particularly when the $12,000-a-year job offers little
satisfaction other than the attendant paycheck, and
fatherhood seems to end a man's youth before he has
had the time to enjoy it. Education, challenging careers, desire to travel or merely to explore the varied
styles of life which his vocation makes possible—all
these options may be closed off, sacrificed to the fear
of being ticketed a psychological misfit for failure to
meet the contemporary notion of male normality:
prompt settling into the groove of family life.

We hear much about the "trapped housewife," the young woman with a college degree or some professional training and experience, who has assumed the burdensome routine of keeping house and rearing several children with no help but adolescent baby-sitters and appliances designed to get out of order. But hers is a shared trap; her husband must cope with competition outside his home *and* her discontent within it. Her demands, social and sexual, are forthright and grow stronger as she, too, feels that she has taken on a burden in marrying—and this though she wanted to marry, or at least feared not to marry.

Can the contemporary male meet the demands which contemporary American existence puts upon him? Especially when those demands are increasingly exacting? Look, for example, at this advertisement: "Mavest styles sport coats for men who are witty, sincere, passionate, heroic, intellectual, sophisticated, dynamic, creative, introspective, intense, successful— and also the guy next door." Even if it was written with tongue in cheek, this bit of advertising copy shows how the American male is expected to add to the virtues of inner-direction some characteristic virtues of other-direction. He must embody these contradictory qualities and show rugged strength besides. Hence the all but pathological concern with display of masculinity, with sports (often merely with the watching of sports), with boating, fishing, and hunting, with garments properly rugged,[7] with all the trappings of a kind of male activity which modern mechanization has made all but obsolete. Above all, men must act the male; they must assert themselves at home and at work. In the nineteenth century, a man's economic adequacy and social assertiveness were taken for granted; he was not obliged to impress anyone except by his achievements. Today he must show himself a man to his peers[8]—and those now include wife and even children, for the middle-class family has become democratized: children speak; they make their wishes heard; they have the capacity to make their father feel incompetent, unequal to meet their needs and therefore impotent.[9] Since the mores of the middle class rapidly affect all levels of American society, changes in the middle class are not restricted to that social group. Even traditionally patriarchal people like the Italian peasant immigrants are, in their contemporary descendants, beginning to show evidence that the position of the father has changed and that the mother has taken on a new role in the family.

The notion of the dominant mother has become almost a cliché in discussion of the American family, and she does indeed exist. But how has she become dominant? Largely because the American husband and father has removed himself from home and family. Concentration on work and leaving family discipline, for example, to the mother is not new in the United States, of course, but its results have become more noticeable. The post-Freudian American woman has at once accepted the role of housewife and mother and rejected it. Women who are aware that life offers them other possibilities than mixing casseroles and wiping noses may well resent both the limits imposed by the role they have chosen and the need to function as family guide, director, and disciplinarian. Consequently, they may become more exacting.

The relative decline of the male position in the American family further intensifies the threat to his psychological security. Economically and socially, he faces danger, a danger which may readily be apprehended in sexual terms. The therapist is well aware of the deep roots of men's fear of the female: the fanged vagina is an ancient folklore motif; the wicked stepmother figures largely in fairly tales; the enmity between Hera and Heracles may go far deeper than the surface tension between a betrayed wife and the son of her husband's mistress. In contemporary America,

I think they're the losers. People
used to have time of their own when
they could sit and daydream, sit
and think, rather than be on the
go all the time.
                    —Father of three
                    quoted in *Newsweek*

Modern youth becomes the dreaded
avenging angel of his parents, since
he holds the power to prove his
parents' success or failure as parents. . . .
            —BRUNO BETTELHEIM

CHAPTER THREE

Growing Up Male:
The American Man As Son

Growing up male is a difficult job. Growing up male in America is made even more difficult because it must go on in a swiftly changing society where the structure of the family has altered and the position of the son has been seriously modified. The adolescent boy in contemporary America is, in some respects, treated as an adult even before he has experienced the traditional *Sturm und Drang* of the late teens. Yet in other respects, he is exiled from society, confined, especially if he belongs to the middle class, to an affluent ghetto.[1] An observer who restricts his view to the current scene may consider precocity to be a peculiarly contemporary aspect of "growing up male" in the United States. Looking backward, however, one sees that prosperous youths usually have been segregated in school or college. And ever since Europeans have recorded their observations of American society, they have contrasted the brash self-sufficiency of American young men with the modest deference European middle-class boys showed their elders.

Buying Identity

Reuel Denney attributes the singular character of today's adolescent's being treated as an adult to his recently acquired ability to buy. But ever since the eighteenth century, when the Eastern seaboard of North America was still a British colony, the young

American has been able to earn money; in Denney's phrase, he has been able to buy as an adult. Today, however, the adolescent's income is more completely disposable; he is not generally expected to contribute to the family income. Parents provide the essentials; his earnings are his own and these highly disposable earnings constitute the teenage market which merchandizing experts and advertisers keep under continuous and peculiar siege.

Basically, however, that market is merely an aspect of an adult market where goods are bought as much to fill psychic as physical needs. In its explanation of the world of the teenager *Newsweek* discovered that it was when shopping that he was most likely to feel "mature, independent, good, and happy." [2] It would be interesting to find out whether this was true of his elders. Certainly, women have long been pictured as soothing unhappiness with new hats. Their husbands may buy consolation in cars as well as bottles. And both can charge their purchases, a privilege which is only beginning to be granted the adolescent. He still usually must pay cash for what he buys, whereas his elders no longer find cash essential. Indeed, in buying an automobile, a customer ready to pay cash may not be at all to the seller's taste because so large a share of his total profit comes from financing the customer's purchase. "Buy now and pay later" lures from every side and for every kind of expenditure, from a college education or a trip to Europe to the third TV set necessary for truly "gracious living." "Grow up now and pay later," Denney writes, might well have been the motto of "the youth who quickly spent a fantasy four thousand on a credit-card spree." [3]

"Grow up now and pay later" has a far more general significance: it aptly describes the situation of young American males who are encouraged to seek some kinds of adult experience and, at the same time, are discouraged from others. In *Growing Up Absurd,* Paul

Goodman says that there is no "American" family, any more than there is an "American" science. There is, however, an "American" language, an American system of education, an American pattern of business, a community environment which the child encounters as he ventures from home to confront the world.[4]

The Irrelevant Past

It is this environment which is marked by change, change so rapid that it makes past experience irrelevant; and it is in this environment that American boys grow up. At this point, a European might murmur some objection to such readiness to discard the past, but few contemporary Americans see much need for any reservation. What has the American experience of the peasant immigrant from Ireland, Germany, Italy, Greece, or the stretch of Slavic Europe, to do with the American world in which his grandsons live? What signposts for today's young men are offered by the world of the 1920's or the early 1930's when their parents were reared? In Kenneth Keniston's telling phrase, the upward mobility of individuals ". . . is but a part of that collective social mobility which has characterized Americans as a nation, [which] brings shifts in values, technologies, and patterns of life" so drastic and so swift as to ". . . suggest to many youths that there *are* no values, institutions, or ways of life that withstand the tests of time."[5]

The irrelevance of past and especially of parents' experience is illustrated and perhaps intensified by the example of indifferent or ineffectual fathers. The modern American family has been reduced to its biological nucleus, parents and children, with all that reduction means in the way of attention and emotion concentrated (particularly by the mother) on a few children. For although the one-child family may be less common now than during the 1920's and 1930's, few

middle-class non-Catholic American families count as
many children as was the rule during the nineteenth
century.

In the traditional European family setting, the son
had a significant and rather stable position, one which
tended to support the boy in his striving to develop a
reasonably secure identity. The eldest son especially
was charged with a range of expectations and endowed
with a set of privileges. He was expected to maintain,
and perhaps to improve, the family's position in society.
He enjoyed a privileged place in respect to mother
and siblings, and closeness to the father was reckoned as part of that privilege. Often, the eldest son
would follow his father's occupation, succeeding to
his practice if he were a doctor or lawyer, or taking
his place in business, whether in a family-owned enterprise or in the same firm where the father had
worked or in which he had risen. Ultimately, the eldest
son would inherit a major share of the family possessions—and also a set of responsibilities for the care
of mother and siblings after the father's death.

This type of family setting gave sons—oldest or
only sons particularly—a fairly close relationship with
their father, whether that relationship was friendly or
antagonistic. Consider an English example, John Addington Symonds, Victorian critic and cultural his-
torian, and his father. Dr. John Symonds was a Victorian father in the tradition of prosperous, British
nineteenth-century nonconformity, liberal in religion,
earnest in pursuit of culture, devoted preacher of the
Gospel of Work, affectionate in a nondemonstrative
way, intensely directive—he would not allow his son to
acquire the unmanly accomplishment of playing the
piano—yet willing to reinforce the boy's physical weakness by an all too intense concern for his health. Father
and son were almost oppressively close. When the
elder Symonds died, his son wrote that he had lost
his best friend, who combined "spontaneous and un-

selfish love" with "sympathy for my tastes and occupations, pride in my success if I ever had any, interest in every undertaking, jealous care of every interest." Yet only when that jealous care no longer scrutinized every aspect of his life could Symonds begin the large-scale studies in Italian cultural history for which he is remembered. In spite of his appreciation of his father as a truly manly and powerful figure, for all his desire to meet his father's expectations of him, Symonds seems to have felt his father, while he lived, as a thwarting, frustrating presence.⁶

In another cultural context, consider the brief but significant relationship between André Gide and his father, a relationship which we glimpsed earlier, seeing the son as awed observer of his father's importance in a remote world. Freud and his father had an interesting relationship, too, and one which Freud may well have used as material for his own theory of the development of the psychological structure of the family.

George Groddeck, whom Freud claimed as a psychoanalyst although Groddeck had no analytic training and even, as he admitted, had been willing to condemn psychoanalysis before he gave it a real hearing, shows another aspect of the older European pattern of father-son relationship.⁷ Groddeck's father (like Symonds', a doctor) chose his son's profession when the boy was only three, but where Symonds lost his mother when he was not yet five years old, Groddeck's mother was critically present, constantly comparing her husband to her father, and always to her husband's disparagement. Yet she did not try to interfere with his direction of their son's life, and Groddeck remembered his father's strength, his wisdom, his affection—and his sternness. When the elder Groddeck burst into anger, his wife yielded; the father took command. When Groddeck's father died, he put his father's idol, Ernst Schweniger, in his place; later Groddeck tried to replace that idol with Freud (a position Freud refused, incidentally).[8]

A more recent instance of the influence of father on son is provided by the Kafkas. Franz Kafka himself, according to his biographer, Max Brod, seems always to have resisted any Freudian interpretation of his problem, but the facts speak louder than the novelist's resistance: the elder Kafka so overwhelmed his gifted son that the latter seems to have been suffocated, his life quenched by a disease of the lungs which seems to have been, in large part, of psychic origin.[9]

If we turn from life to the novel, a literary form which seeks, in a variety of ways, to express the experience of life, we see a curious movement in the English literature which so long helped to shape American attitudes. During the late eighteenth and early nineteenth centuries, filial piety was fashionable;[10] the son was supposed to be submissive. Gradually, sentiment changed; rebellion against the father became a literary cliché. Sometimes, as Howard Wolf points out in referring to the work of D. H. Lawrence, that rebellion turned the son toward his mother.[11] Again, as in Samuel Butler's *The Way of All Flesh*, rebellion assailed both parents. Butler, writing long before Freud began working, although the novel was not published until 1903, presents a version of the "family romance" in Victorian England which portrays in the harshest light the father-son relationship that existed in the inner-directed nineteenth century. He shows us a self-made man, George Pontifex, thrashing his sons "two or three times a week and some weeks a good deal oftener, but in those days fathers were always thrashing their boys," scolding them for ingratitude, pitting one against the other in the matter of pocket money, manipulating their inheritance, and constantly threatening to cut them out of the will. George's son, whom Butler is said to have modeled after his own clergyman father, went on in the same good way, raised his children unspoiled by sparing of the rod, so that his twelve-year-old knew that "he did not love his papa and mamma, in spite of all their goodness both in themselves and to him. He hated papa, and did not like mamma, and this was what none but a bad and ungrateful boy would do after all that had been done for him." [12]

Butler's novel marks a new departure; he is one of the first English novelists to cast aside the tradition of respect and affection for parents—fathers particularly —and to take it for granted that middle-class fathers and mothers abuse their children, psychologically if not physically. Further, in any conflict between the younger and older generations, the younger is always right.

In the contemporary middle-class American family, Butler's viewpoint seems to prevail: duty, if so old-fashioned a word may be used, runs from parents to children, not in the other direction. This reversal of sentiment is paralleled by a shift in parental roles, and consequently a change in the role of the son. The Victorian woman considered herself to be wife and mother; her husband came first. In the contemporary American family, the woman is likely to consider herself to be mother and wife, in that order. When a marriage is broken, children go to her almost as a matter of course; only in exceptional instances is any mother regarded as unfit to have custody of her children. Everyone is familiar with the economic reasons for the father's frequent absence from the home and the mother's increasingly important place in it. Even in suburbia, where "togetherness" is supposed to rule, fathers are often psychologically as well as physically absent. Many a man may consider his checkbook to be his principal tie to his son: a father does all that can be decently expected when he pays the bills. If he gives a few weekend hours to games with his

children or a vacation week to a camping trip with
his sons, many a middle-class father[13] thinks his whole
duty as a parent better than well done. "Understanding" is for mothers—or psychotherapists.

The Disappearance of Adult Models

As fathers become separated from their sons, younger males find that the structure of the contemporary
American family (and indeed of contemporary American society) has all but excluded useful male substitutes for the father. The parent-surrogates, who
have become important in many children's lives,[14] fill
some of the need but not all of it.

Contemporary parent-surrogates are more or less
professional; they are not a modern version of the
situation, so often described by anthropologists, where
tribal elders, and especially the mother's brother,
"made" the youth into an adult male. We have no
real tribal elders in America, even in the shape of
grandfathers, uncles, and older cousins. Once, in smaller communities, the boy might have found, outside the
family circle, some older male friend, confidant, and
model in a local storekeeper, mechanic, or even town
"character." Most American families live in their own
homes, which means in suburban rather than urban
areas; and suburbs today have become so much the
single-class dormitory separated from the larger context of economic and social life that contemporary
boys may well have fewer opportunities for informal
association with a variety of adult men than did their
fathers and grandfathers.

Contemporary middle-class communities are often
too limited, then, and family ties too tenuous to allow
the development of what one might call the *natural*
father-surrogate. Even if family ties are maintained,
they often are a source of conflict rather than an
aspect of education and a form of psychological sup-

port. For, it must be said again that, instead of serving as a body of material which can assist with their education, the experiences of an older generation become a barrier against communication with young people. From many sources, we hear that the past is merely something that has happened, that it has nothing to say to the present. Artists continue to want to destroy the museums and even to assert that each decade produces all the art that can be relevant to its experience and its existence. Sociologists like Daniel Bell and the publicists who present the work of scholars to a wider public declare that current ideologies are merely phrases mechanically repeated: capitalism, communism, socialism, nationalism, freedom, regimentation, individualism—empty babble all.[15] The contemporary world is made by technology. And technology (as such publicists generally do not say) has achieved take-off. Like the media Marshall McLuhan describes, technology develops of itself, ungovernably, with no purpose that people traditionally reared can recognize as related to real human needs. Even historians publicly wonder whether their discipline is worth pursuing: what can knowledge of the past tell twentieth-century man about himself?

The Transformation of Parents

The situation just described is further complicated for young males by the character of the relationship between parents, and particularly by the readiness of many parents to make their children parties to their own conflicts. We hear a great deal about the need for democratic family relations, about the value of the nonauthoritarian attitudes and the propriety of treating children as equals. Certainly, the presumption that parents are invariably wise, merely because they are parents, with the accompanying demand for obedient deference has little to recommend it; that attitude made miserable the lives of too many nine-teenth-century children. Certainly, too, the attempt to conceal from children the inevitable friction which arises between parents can lead only to parental hy-pocrisy and great stress for children thus "protected." But making them participants in their parents' con-flicts has evil results of its own. Frequently, the child —in this case the son—is invited to take part in a family decision: shall they buy a boat or perhaps shall they spend a summer vacation driving cross-country or spend it at a lake resort? But the parents are actual-ly striving for dominance, a striving which well may have very strong sexual undertones. In such a situation, the child becomes both tool and bone of contention; he is, in effect, asked to take sides in contentions not of his making and to pass judgments he is not quali-fied to pronounce.

By bringing sons into this sort of family partner-ship, parents destroy a necessary image of themselves and surround the pattern of family behavior with an atmosphere of falsity. Children are not their parents' equals, in the sense of having equivalent status. Nor are children capable of sharing the kind of problems which are the peculiar consequences of the relation-ship between husband and wife. Certain family prob-lems can and indeed should be communicated to chil-dren. Even young sons can understand the economic facts of their family's life, and those facts can be presented in ways which need not undermine a son's conviction that his father is a worthy person with whom he can identify. Crises like birth and death, circumstantial changes like shifts of jobs or moves from place to place may be shared with children to their psychological advantage.

Such sharing is very different from embroiling sons in conflicts between parents. Certain notions—we may call them *images*—about parents are useful to children. Mother should be a consoling, quiet mediator between her son and the world, but not possessively protective or aggressively assertive. A dominating, possessive mother tends to distort her son's development (to say nothing of her daughter's), encouraging the formation of neurotic attitudes toward women which will tend to make the boy incapable of genuine emotional involvement with them, unless involvement is rooted in hostility. Father, on the other hand, should be powerful and wise. This does not mean that he is to be authoritarian and domineering in the style Samuel Butler portrayed, or more subtly dominating as was the elder Symonds. The modern world has no place for such a father figure and its contribution to a son's neurotic development. But children continue to need a father who takes a leading place in the family, a father who cares, who sets the pace for his son and gives him sufficient material to begin building the psychological structure of male identity.

Sons and Fathers

From what the psychotherapist sees in his practice, contemporary American fathers do not provide that material. Clinical experience shows the existence of a singular emptiness in relationships between parents and sons. Fathers are often so detached from their families, so absorbed in their own concern with business or professional success, that their sons do not develop even a forthright antagonism for them, let alone a close positive relationship. In the nineteenth century, and earlier, a son might be brutalized, subjected to the tyranny of parental authority, to physical abuse or economic exploitation. In colonial America, for example, it was not uncommon for a young man to demonstrate that he had come to his majority by knocking down his father when the older man tried to discipline him with fists or club. The youth would leave the family farm then and go off to earn a living

on his own. We can scarcely cite this as an example
of a desirable relationship between father and son,
but it was surely a real relationship—and one out of
which a son could develop an awareness of his identity.
In that situation of intimacy and anger, a son might
grow up to hate his father, but he would at least
know what constituted one version of a man. (And
in the irony of existence, he might proceed to do
with his son as he had been done by.)

In the contemporary encounter between son and
father, old-fashioned brutal domination may be rare,
but there also seems a notable absence of real and
genuine fellowship, of what my native Dutch calls
gemeenschappelijk gebeuren (the sharing of a significant experience), a phrase still almost impossible to
translate, which connotes those deep genuine feelings
which people share with one another. As I have said
elsewhere,[16] such feelings may be expressed in what
may appear rather trivial behavior—so small a matter
as two people strolling down a street together. One
sunny Saturday morning, as I made my way down a
busy street in Amsterdam, I became aware of a number of fathers walking along with their sons, mostly
eight- to twelve-year-olds, and talking about the things
they passed. The free Saturday morning is new in
Holland (where most people have, until recently,
worked half a day on Saturday) and is a much cherished bit of leisure, hours which might be spent cultivating a garden, for instance, or doing small necessary repairs. But many a Dutch father chooses to spend
this free time with his son. Americans of similar
social standing might find walking an odd form of
diversion, but it is the sharing of leisure in such un-
planned, intimate fashion that is significant, not the
manner of that sharing.

The American family is no longer a really close-
knit unit, we hear, and this situation, too, is the outcome of contemporary technological and economic

developments. Granted; yet one wonders whether such changes must necessarily operate to block genuine human relations between parents and children. Such distortions of relationships should scarcely be accepted as matter of course; rather, they require comprehensive social self-analysis. One might even question the value of the kinds of social and technological development which produce such warping of relationships: rephrasing the Scriptural question: Was man made for technology or technology for man?

In any society, the relationship of the young male (and the female, too) to the father figure is of crucial significance. The father is the first man in the life of any contemporary American middle-class child; and in a boy's early years, he is *the* male figure. A son reports his father's accomplishments to his friends, boasts about his father's strength or skill or possessions, seeks to fashion himself on the model his father offers. If father is so often absent, so distant, that he appears principally as a dutiful provider of things, if he is seen chiefly as the troubled and often inadequate authority figure at home, the son has little to build on—or toward—except, perhaps a sense of alienation. When a son feels his father to be insecure or weak, the boy suffers. Dick Hendrikse, a young Dutch novelist, reports a youth's disillusion with what he interprets to be his father's weakness (and a man's understanding of what that appearance had really signified):

I received the news of the Dutch surrender just like any fifteen-year-old who hears that his football club has been beaten. No less, but also no more than that. I did not know what war was and meant. I did not know the consequences. And then when the speaker over the radio had finished the announcement of our surrender I heard a strange noise. My father, my great, strong, hardworking father kept his face in his hands and cried like a child. Nobody said anything and I was very much ashamed. Because I was fifteen years old and at that age you consider it childish when a grown-up man cries with long and intense sobs. I believe, if I remember it well, that at that moment I despised my father. A boy of fifteen can be cruel in his ignorance. I did not understand why my father cried that day. Now, twenty-five years later, I am proud of him. Because he cried, since he understood that the war had not ended with that radio announcement.[17]

In the contemporary American family, although the son may not feel close to the father, he does feel that, like the all too present Victorian papa, the older man demands that his boy "make good." The specific content of "making good" may differ, but most middle-class fathers (and many in the lower-income groups) expect their sons to "do better" than they themselves have done, to achieve greater prosperity and higher status. In this sense, fathers not only see their sons as competitors but encourage them to compete and seek to help them succeed in the competition. Where making good requires that the son excel in athletics, the father may pay for expensive equipment and coaching. Where the son is to make good economically, the father will seek to provide education or useful acquaintances, or even capital. And to acquire the means of procuring these, the father may spend so much time and effort at work that he becomes all but a stranger to his son.[18]

Peers as Guides: Youth Culture

Making good may also require that, to satisfy his father's expectations, a son stand well with his peers. Here we strike another aspect of the problem of growing up male in contemporary America: where parents and parent-surrogates falter, the peer group moves in. Increasingly, children between nine and fifteen years old tend to rely on their age-mates for direction.

Again, such a movement outward from the exclusive authority of the family toward the sanctions of school and playmates is not novel. Significantly new, however, is the degree of adult acceptance of the peer group as a valid source of standards. Instead of being fondly amused by adolescent conformity and adolescent fads, adults study seriously (sometimes on the practical level of seeking to profit from adolescent spending power) and even imitate them.[19] The world of the middle-class child is cleaner and more orderly than the world of the streets where so many immigrant children grew up; its prospect is far better than that street world of many a contemporary urban Negro child. Yet the middle-class child's world is similarly divorced from home as authority and source of values. School, work, sports, sex, study, jobs after school or in summer, clothes, dating, parties, choice of language and of friends, even the level of vocational aspiration—all these are shaped as much by peers as by parents.[20] Parents continue to pay most of the bills, but we do not often hear of their using command of the family income as a means of making their wills or their values prevail above those of the peer group.

That young people should need to express a wish for parental guidance may seem strange in the light of history. Stranger still are the newspaper accounts of suburban mothers and fathers formally gathered to draft "codes" of teenage behavior, so that the argument "Tom's parents give (let) him" does not become an instrument by which the adolescent can rule his father and mother.

In default of parental action and example, the young male is thrown on his psychological resources. But he has all too few of these. An absent father (and the contemporary father tends to be at least a psychological absentee) makes it difficult for his son to move toward achieving maturity either by identifying or by rejecting him. Father-surrogates rarely give the young man enough support to enable him to form a firm conception of what he wants to become (or, as important, of what he does not want to become). In this situation, the youth turns to his peer group, but his contemporaries are as confused and, in a very real sense, as deprived as he.

For American adolescents not only seem to exist apart from adult society, they are all but banished from it. Accounts of many primitive peoples describe the life which young men led together, apart from the tribe, between puberty and marriage. This was a socially defined segment of the total life experience which trained youths for their adult future. Modern society moves too fast and changes too radically for any such comfortable partitioning of life. Contemporary youth has developed a distinctive culture that is encapsulated, unconnected with what went before and with little organic relation to what will come after. This is especially true, perhaps, of those for whom the economy seems to have comparatively little need, young males who do not appear sufficiently talented for professional or technical training and who are not suitable candidates for certain occupations because they do not match in color or build the "image" of the "rising young executive," "the productive salesman," or the "hard-hitting decision maker." (Where advancement in business is concerned, the youth culture may be relevant to the adult world because friendships and acquaintances established in adolescence can be useful later in corporate settings where "contacts" may be more important than products.)

The distinctive "teenage" culture which has developed in America is not significant because of its novelty but rather because of the role it now appears to play in American life. It bridges adolescence and adulthood, according to Kenneth Keniston, and gives young males an opportunity to develop a sense of identity as they postpone adulthood.[21] This culture imposes claims without accepting corresponding responsibilities. Hence it is a culture of privilege: the middle-class youth usually retains his earnings (although he may be expected to use at least part of them to pay for his own education); he cannot generally be made to pay his debts since, legally, he can conclude only a limited number of contracts; and in many states he is not held to answer for offenses against the law with the same rigor as an adult (in this respect, even the lower-class non-white boy may share in the privileged culture).

Yet growing up male in this teenage culture means growing up in crisis. Adolescence itself is no longer clearly defined. Childhood ends abruptly and it seems to be cut off earlier and earlier, leaving youngsters frustrated. Many are dissatisfied with what their childhood has given them. Abundantly provided, they feel deprived. They enter on physical puberty, which may be taken as the sign of adolescence, and engage in what Erik Erikson calls "discontented search."

It is clear that societies offer any number of ritual combinations of ideological perspective and vigorous movement (dance, sports, parades, demonstrations, riots) to harness youth in the service of their historical aims; and that, where societies fail to do so, these patterns will seek their own combinations, in small groups occupied with serious games, good-natured foolishness, cruel prankishness, and delinquent warfare. In no other stage of the life cycle, then, are the promise of finding oneself and the threat of losing oneself so closely allied.[22]

In America's youth culture, the young male is free to move in all the ways Erikson lists, and the boy enjoys certain real privileges. Yet one privilege he does not generally have: whatever aspect of childhood was carefree, the middle-class adolescent can no longer feel free of care. (This is true for girls as well; they must make ready to join the husband hunt.) The young man must prove himself sexually while he is also equipping himself for life in a market-oriented society where, whatever his chosen vocation, his status will be measured by his ability to buy. Pastimes take on a new meaning accordingly; the young male finds it necessary to participate in competitive team sports and in social activities where competition may be even more intense. Boys as well as girls strive for popularity; rival each other in dating; experiment with sex as another form of competition. Quiet play, spontaneous intimacy with parents and relatives, are less and less common. The contemporary young American male seems to lack capacity for such behavior. His mind's eye turns outward. He identifies with his peer group; he conforms. At times, while conforming, he tries to stand out, to do what everyone else does, but more efficiently, more conspicuously. In none of the things he does, however, can he maintain emotional continuity with the child he was.

As the adolescent male feels this disruption of his experience, he becomes increasingly concerned with appearing to be a man. He must maintain a tight guard against any feelings of affection for his friends or for other males in general. His development as a male thus proceeds in an atmosphere of strain. In his social environment, tension is the norm, whether international politics be in question or an economy striving for perpetual growth and therefore committed to unremitting and rapid change. In the family, further tension is generated by the crisis in parenthood where father and mother make but an uneasy effort to come to terms with their relationship to their children, a relationship which society no longer prescribes. Declining parental authority has not generally been replaced by a sense of intimacy between parents and children. The parent-as-pal notion is recognized as a cliché. The possessive parent (the possessive mother especially) has been the target of so much abuse that many an other-directed person (and the contemporary middle-class American adult is apt to be other-directed) is afraid to show the depth of his concern for an adolescent male child. Young people are urged to bring their problems to their parents, but less than ever do parents seem either appropriate confidants or useful counselors.

The young male, thus unable to resolve his identity problem at home, takes it to school where he hopes to find parent-surrogates in teachers. But their authority, too, is diminishing, and only rarely are approaches to intimacy possible in the large high schools where most young American males get their secondary education. The peer group does possess some of the authority which parents and their surrogates have lost, but one may question its real capacity to further the adolescent male's search for identity. How are people who are likely to lack secure identities themselves to help each other in the journey toward self-discovery? If we regard the peer group as an institution rather than an assemblage of persons, the question may have a more meaningful answer, but is the peer group an institution? Does it, among adolescent male Americans, fulfil a function equivalent to that of the age-grade societies which, in primitive cultures, help young males move from childhood through youth into the skills, privileges, and responsibilities of adulthood?

A number of sociologists, of whom Bennett M.

Berger may be representative,[23] argue that the adolescent peer group and the peculiar youth culture of which it is a part fulfil quite another function: they do not prepare the young male to become a man; rather they reconcile him to accepting a postponement of his demand that he be recognized as an adult.

Our technologically based economy and society require trained personnel. While these people are getting the necessary training—a training which appears to take more and more time—they cannot "earn their keep," however many opportunities there may be to acquire pocket money. Thus the adolescent, as it has been said, is both the spoiled darling and the exile of American society; his singular youth culture operates as a substitute for meaningful functioning in reality. Very largely, that culture is not of youth's making. Rather it is the product of the mass media seeking to market the output of the clothing, cosmetics, and record manufacturers. Financial pages report the millions teenagers spend; promoters devise "junior credit cards" which will circumvent the minor's inability to make valid contracts. The young male is effectively taught how to fill his adult role as a consumer, but he is not attaining adulthood. His unresolved relationships with his parents, his basically unconfronted relationships with his society make him only more inclined to avoid becoming part of the adult world. Avoidance may continue: even after adolescence is chronologically passé the male may continue to behave like an adolescent.[24]

As he approaches adulthood, the young male often feels alienated from himself and from society. It might be more to the point to say that youth feels an absence of, rather than an alienation from, self because his inability to identify with his father or an adequate father-surrogate has made it difficult or even impossible for him to build up his sense of manhood. Society demands that he "be a man," but social impera-

tives are of little help in fulfilling society's requirements. Contemporary society asks the youth to practice contradiction, to be a competitive teammate, a
conforming individualist, a sexual athlete who has
meaningful relationships with all his conquests, a devoted father whose family is likely to include the
children of other marriages, a proponent of peace and
international cooperation who lives in an economy
which draws a sizable proportion of its income from
preparation for war.

Increasingly, the young male faced by these contradictions experiences loneliness and isolation, as
described so tellingly by Kenneth Keniston in "Inburn:
An American Ishmael." [25] In interviews, this young
man reported himself admiring very few people—
exiles like Chopin, lone-wolf artists like Hemingway,
Alexander the Great, perhaps—and disliking many.
From his fellowmen, he expected "hostility, injustice,
. . . slander, abuse." He loathed all that was compla-
cently middle class, yet he could think of no alternative worth striving for. His earthly paradise was the
womb—to which no man can return.

As Keniston pursued his research, he discovered
there were many like Inburn, young men who were
intelligent, sometimes even talented, who came from
homes which were reasonably comfortable economically, who enjoyed "the advantages," but who were,
nevertheless, more than unhappy; they were alienated,
angry and contemptuous sometimes, often completely
detached. For them, life was truly "sound and fury,
signifying nothing." [26]

No psychotherapist who carries his professional
awareness into his ordinary social life will regard
Keniston's young men as exceptional. There is a growing lack of intimacy in American life; especially among
young men intimacy has become something to be
feared. Youths are afraid of genuine encounters; they
avoid relationships, perhaps because they suspect

that these will reveal how weak is their grasp on their identity. The young male must keep men at an emotional distance because his adolescent sexual problems have not been fully faced: he wants to be both masculine and passive—and this in a culture which identifies masculinity with a high degree of competitive aggressiveness. He cannot approach women intimately, either because he fears that in any but a casual sexual relationship, the woman will dominate as his mother so often has dominated—and the American young man fears (and unconsciously desires) no one more than "the girl just like the girl that married dear old Dad."

In my opinion, the absence of meaningful appropriate intimacy between son and parents, and especially between son and father, is important in encouraging the early marriages that are becoming common in our middle class. Pseudo-adult sexual encounters and marriages are both a result of the sons' being deprived of the pleasures *and* the trials of a slower passage through boyhood and adolescence, leading more surely to real adulthood.

Estrangement

Historians have long told how differences between a king and the prince who was his heir sharpened political conflicts and shaped political groupings. In eighteenth-century Britain, for example, this helped to make George III the man he was and contributed to the American revolution. Literature describes the father-son conflict on many levels, from the myth of Chronos emasculated and slain to the struggle which one kind of romantic hero fought in order to emancipate himself from a bourgeois family and its business or profession and to fulfil himself as an artist. The conflict has grown more acute in a country where social change proceeds at a pace so swift that even a middle-aged person may find it difficult to realize the continuity between the world in which he lives and the world of a few decades ago, in which his attitudes were shaped. The son has very little understanding of his father's motivations, and it is exceedingly difficult for him to learn "what makes the old man tick" since the "old man" himself may not know. He is so caught up in the problems of adjusting to change that he tends to lose interest in, and real emotional contact with, his own past. Fathers are thus less able to give their sons a sense of continuity by helping them become rooted in family experience.

Yet many American parents believe they should be their children's friends; some say they want their sons' confidence, many even think they do have it. Nevertheless, and in spite of the slogans of "palship," estrangement between fathers and sons has led to a breakdown in communication. The two have always lived in separate, even antagonistic worlds, but they have also always lived in a world that was intimately shared. This common portion of life has shrunk in America; the separated areas are not only larger, they seem more separate. Consequently, the traditional conflict between the generations has taken on a new dimension. It has passed beyond the stage where, like Ibsen's Master Builder, the older generation feared that the younger would rob it of privileges and possessions. Now we see the passing of even the connection which that fear implied. The middle-class son stands at a psychological distance from his father; his concept of masculinity has changed. No longer does the sixteen-year-old boy try to look and behave as differently as he can from the girl his age. The current adolescent does not *feel* emasculated—he leaves that to his father; the adolescent sees himself as different from the traditional kind of masculine male. He may even, like the stringy-haired young woman pictured in *Holiday*, have cut sex down to size.[27] Sex no longer has the compulsive attractiveness of the taboo. Sexuality may be a source of pleasure but it seems to have lost its function as a final determinator of masculinity.

The lower-class son may be separated from family and father on another level: quite often, even in European countries, higher education takes young men out of their father's social class. A European may feel that such obvious social mobility is dangerous to psychological health,[28] but in the United States even official policy is directed toward encouraging it. From the kindergarten on, we attempt to encourage the children of the poor to aspire not only to get jobs, but through education to equip themselves to leave their parents' social world and enter what is actually an alien culture.

On whatever level it exists, from whatever source it arises, the gulf between the generations seems, if not deeper, at least more evident than before. Earlier, youths may have quarreled with fathers, attacked their value systems, rebelled against their authority, but such youths did not dismiss their fathers as irrelevant. This situation seems the more strange because so many American parents are ardent worshippers in the cult of youth. As the son seeks a kind of pseudo-adulthood, the father in much of his behavior seems to be striving to achieve a pseudo-youth. He rejects the parental role on another level: he not only often deprives the family of his genuine presence, he may also refuse to accept himself as an adult.

Raised by fathers who have not grown up, it is easy to understand why a significant number of young American males see the adult role not as something to be sought but as something to be evaded, since it demands commitment to middle-class values that appear empty and absurd to them. The bureaucratic world of business or government is oppressively stratified and becoming more so; Paul Goodman calls it a

"closed room with a rat race going on in the middle."
And the rats apparently are running after a prize that,
to some, seems of diminishing worth: money and what
money will buy are necessary, but they cannot, of
themselves, give joy to life. Even the world of the independent professional appears no more genuinely
stimulating than the realm of the bureaucrat. Money,
too, is the goal of that world which often is tributary
to the corporation.

But repudiating that world often seems to offer the
young male no better reason for commitment. Art
is a problematical alternative. The artist engages his
deepest self in a continuous battle with his material
as he tries to realize his vision. He recognizes durable
and valid challenges in his work, but he is wary, for
he has seen the mass media seduce many a wild
talent. Ideologies have little emotional hold; even
the half-educated have learned to see through them.
The struggle for civil rights has given young men a
large chance to prove themselves, but comparatively
few have chosen this way to rise above the rut of
alienation. The fantasies of the far right give other
young men scope for their paranoia. Yet, isolation
and disaffectation seem easier than commitment to art
or ideals. Many a youth ultimately dons the mask of
the gregarious, "outgoing" competitor, but until mask
and self merge (as they often do), he suffers; he
knows that he does not know who he is. Other young
males are less ready, or less able, to don the mask.
They are the adolescents who refuse to pledge allegiance to adult values. They are the juvenile delinquents. They are the students who prolong their university sojourn through several degrees and as many
fellowships as they can acquire. They *were* the beats
(who are definitely *out* now!). Even after they have
become chronologically adult, they cling to adolescent
attitudes.

Surviving Youth

Does the foregoing description of the young American male in transit between adolescence and adulthood apply to people outside the great cities? In my own experience, the Midwesterner is not so strikingly different from his young male counterpart in Boston or New York. A distinctive, widespread youth culture has emerged in the United States. Certain aspects of experience affect most contemporary middle-class youths. Their parents are apparently more neurotic and less competent to fill their own difficult role than they were a couple of generations ago; hence the young male is affected by indifference or hostility to a mother seen as dominating and a father perceived as inadequate. The youth senses the discontinuity in his life, the break between a childhood which has been hurried through rather than lived out, and an adolescence which lacks definition. Often, such a youth is troubled by the awareness that his father is still searching for security in his relation to his society, his wife and his own identity. As the boy learns to know himself as a son in a family setting, he also learns to know his parents, not as persons who serve as models of adulthood, but as troubled individuals to whom he finds it difficult to relate. Mother and father both are caught in a net of problems, financial, social, and psychological, and these, by no means new in kind, are nonetheless particularly burdensome in our complex society.

The social distresses of parents further tangle their relationship with their children. In this kind of family setting, the son is in an unenviable position. He must strive for some sense of identity, but his swiftly changing environment does not give him the time necessary to mature at anything like a manageable pace. In earlier periods, boys acquired the capacity to make

their own choices as a consequence of their relationship to their parents, and especially to fathers who
were examples of what men should be. In today's
American family, the son too often is given neither
leisure nor model: even in his early teens he is expected to act independently, deprived of meaningful
strong relationships with parents who *are* parents
rather than imitation peers.

Freud has taught us that in our adult behavior we
tend continually to renew our relationships with our
parents in various guises and disguises. When a son's
relations with his mother and father become increasingly estranged, empty, distorted—and the psychotherapist sees this situation as characteristic of many
patients under thirty—his relations with other people
are likely to be distorted, too. The son who has been
unable to come to terms with his parents, especially
with his father, will find it particularly difficult to
achieve genuine adulthood.

More and more, the young male is confused about
his sexual and social identity, uncertain about his
personal goals, indifferent to the values that society
presents to him, hence unwilling to commit himself
to relationships (however eager he may be to marry
young) or to ideas. His awareness of the rapidity of
social change adds to his sense of impotence. He is a
stranger and alone in a world he never made—and all
too frequently he is afraid. He feels without power to
rule the course of his own life in a social and political
environment; he feels unable to govern no matter how
often or how loudly he may be told that he lives in a
self-governing democracy. Time itself seems fore-
shortened; how practical are long-range commitments
in a political world that quite conceivably may destroy
itself and him next week—and by accident at that?

Rootless and purposeless at bottom, many a young
man may seem cheerfully to follow the road of least
resistance, conform to the customary patterns of con-

duct, accept his education, prepare for his economic vocation, participate in the social activities of his peers, and behave as he is expected to. Nevertheless, at times, young American males break out—or down. Then we read of prosperous youths acting as vandals, behaving in ways that seem to be part of an *absurd*, senseless rebellion. Or we read of drunkenness, drug addiction, LSD, sexual promiscuity, emotional illness, and other phenomena which reveal psychological instability.[29] The psychotherapist, observing the American scene from the clinician's vantage point, may conclude that growing up male in the United States is extremely difficult; the chance of passing through adolescence without psychological damage is small indeed. The American male generally survives his youth, but too often he is far from prepared to cope with the responsibilities of life as an adult.

Such as the Father is, Such is the Son . . .
the Father Eternal, the Son Eternal.
—THE BIBLE

In Deinem Lehnstuhl regiertest Du die Welt.
[In your armchair you rule the world.]
—FRANZ KAFKA
in *Brief an den Vater*

VOOR VADER

o vader wij zijn samen geweest
in de langzame trein zonder bloemen
die de nacht als een handschoen aan-
en uittrekt wij zijn samen geweest
vader terwijl het donker ons dichtsloeg

waar ben je nu op een klein ritje
in de vrolijke bries van een groene auto
of legde de dag haar handschoen
niet op een tafel waar schemering en

zachte genezing zeker zijn in de toekomst

mijn lippen mijn tedere lippen dicht
                    —HANS LODEIZEN*
                    16 Juli 1950

[FOR FATHER

father we went together
in the slow train without flowers
which the night pulls on and off
like a glove we went together
father while the dark smashed in on us

where you are now on a short ride
in the cheerful breeze of a green car
or did day not lay down her glove
on a table where dusk and soft recovery
were certain to be in the future

my lips my tender lips close]

* Hans Lodeizen was a young Dutch poet, who wrote his poem
a few days before he died at the age of twenty-six of a rare
blood disease in Lausanne in 1950. The translation is by
Richard McConchie.

CHAPTER IV

Disappearing Fathers?

Until now, the American male as father has been discussed from the son's point of view. Here the focus shifts to the father himself. The contemporary American father appears to stand at a crucial stage of development, a moment when tendencies long present and active seem to be reaching a point of culmination.

During the past half-century, but especially since the end of World War II, Americans have been much aware of the changes which have occurred in family life, particularly in what may be called its *power structure*. The emphasis has, however, been placed on the altered position of children and mothers. Society has paid attention to the changing position and role of women; the role and position of men have been taken for granted—as if in a social world made up of two sexes, one could experience a marked change in role without the other's changing, too. This rather naïve attitude is a kind of tribute to the tradition of male dominance: the male is taken as norm; he is presumed to be the stable factor; his social position is fixed.

The presumption is evidently obsolescent although it continues to exist as an unexpressed major premise of much discussion about the social scene in America. It is tempting to speculate how refusing to recognize that the male's position (and particularly that of the father) has indeed altered may lie at the root of certain political trends; surely one can hear such a re-

fusal behind the clamor for return to "basic values,"
to the "good old days" and their good old ways. This
country, some would say, needs not only a good five-
cent cigar, but good strap-wielding fathers in the
home, and good low-tax men in executive mansions.

The Diminishing Father

The old days have gone. The old ways are in flux.
Nowhere is this more evident than in the weakening
position of the father. Once he was pictured as the
authority in the home; now he is portrayed as its butt.
This is not entirely a contemporary phenomenon.
Ever since the United States went from an agricultural
to an industrial economy—beginning as early as the
1830's in the Northeast—father has been a bit of a joke:
his economic mobility outstripped his social adapta-
bility. While wife and children tried to adopt upper-
middle-class manners and tastes, father remained
as he was born, stubbornly lower-middle-class. Seriously, in novels like Howells' *The Rise of Silas Lap-
ham,* jeeringly, in a comic strip like *Bringing Up
Father,* the American *nouveau-riche* father has been
shown to be inept, clumsy, and ill-at-ease in the
world. But smiles and sneers were directed as much
or more toward his social-climbing wife and the
pampered children who wanted to forget the world
they had outgrown, monetarily at least. Father, for
all his naïve informality or outright crudity, stands
firm; he is his old-fashioned self, retaining his established identity, as it were, rather than trying to accommodate himself to the group into which his new
wealth has bought him entry.

In contrast to attitudes which endured until the
1920's, we hear little now of father's stubborn resistance to social grace and aesthetic appreciation. Today, we laugh at father's incapacity to govern his family. No longer does he command attention and def-

erence by the mere sound of his voice. No longer does he exemplify success and achievement.[1] In fiction, particularly in the mass media of comic strip and TV, "Father knows best," is only a sarcasm. He is the person who makes ludicrous blunders, especially in dealing with people, and who is rescued from the consequences of his ineptitude by his wife, or even by his adolescent son or daughter. Father has lost his traditional position in the family structure.

In compensation, perhaps, if anything goes amiss, especially if a child is emotionally disturbed, not the father, but mother is held to blame. Patients in psychotherapy usually assume that their neuroses have grown out of their relationships with their mothers; any mention of father surprises them. In many instances, only after the patient has spent some time in therapy does he begin to talk about his father, whether as a protective or antipathetic figure.[2] What could more vividly illustrate the erosion of the traditional father-son relationship?

Once father was, as a matter of course, guide and model for his son; today, frequently, he neither has that function nor wishes to have it. When Kenneth Keniston looks at the family histories of his alienated young men, he tends to find that they have grown up in families where the father is seen as weak yet oppressive, responsible for confining a potentially talented mother to the dreary round of housewifery. That same "abused" mother manipulates father, nevertheless, so that alienated young men see their fathers to be foolish, false, and weak. Sometimes, fathers seem absorbed in their families, or at least in the houses and cars that they have bought to sustain a "good" life. Just as often, fathers who find their families disappointing as a source of emotional sustenance turn to their work. But that work, however compulsively it may be pursued, often yields only empty barrels for harvest.[3]

In contrast with the European middle-class father, the father in America often has become a stranger in his family. This, too, is no novel trend, but it may seem strange that there should be so much evidence of it at a time when leisure has supposedly increased, when middle-class parents are, by and large, so much younger than they used to be, and when one is deluged with talk about the revival of family living as a consequence of the postwar generation's exodus to the suburbs. Perhaps contemporary leisure is less the case with the middle class than with people at a lower income level. The blue-collar unionized workman and the white-collar office worker both have fixed, and shrinking, work weeks. People in the typical middle-class occupations—business management and the professions—are not protected by union contract, by custom, or by employer willingness to make concessions in order to block unionization: here long hours of work are expected (the three-hour lunch usually is at least nominally in pursuit of business, not relaxation). Often, business and social life are indistinguishable; "deals" are turned on the golf links or at the bridge table or, if certain scandalous reports are to be believed, in expense-account beds.

Images of Maleness

Fathers so occupied have little free time to give their children. Separation between father and son grows; spontaneity in the relationship is depleted by the emphasis on the external signs of masculinity. Fathers can no longer be physically close to their sons even if they do spend time in the boys' company. Again, this is not new: English and American manners have long held tenderness to be somewhat unmanly and have forbidden physical demonstrations of good feelings between men. Even after long separation, Americans shake hands; the formal European kiss of greeting is suspect. Slaps on the back, digs in the ribs, punches are permissible; a quietly encircling arm, however, elicits at least unspoken comment.

On the other hand, and perhaps psychologically related to the convention which forbids the male to show tender emotion except in extreme stress, and certainly not to another male, we see fondness for boxing and football among Americans (one wonders whether the decline of professional wrestling from a genuine contest into a grotesque mock-sadistic exhibition may show fear of even witnessing close bodily contact among men). If people are forbidden to touch in affection, can they approach intimacy when they engage in formalized nonthreatening hostility?

Longtime trends have become stronger in recent decades; an adolescent boy who walks arm-in-arm with his father may be regarded as odd, if not unmanly. On the other hand, fathers who refrain from an overt show of affection for their sons communicate the fear underlying that avoidance. As a result, the son will shun any sort of closeness with other men. Thus at a time when homosexuality seems to be increasing, we see young men all but pathologically afraid to be close to one another.

The Refusal of Fatherhood

In this instance, the father does offer his son a model, but a model of neurotic fear and weakness rather than a model of manliness. The father has abdicated his authority; his wife now governs the home. A man may be willing to accept responsibility at work (although much is heard about the desire to avoid responsibility, even in business), but he prefers not to make decisions for the family. He may become friends with his sons; however, it is an undemanding, surface friendship calling for little intimacy. The father is a pleasant companion, at times, but rarely is he

willing to provide the image of stable maturity that
his sons need if they are to establish a secure, un-
troubled male identity. Such reluctance to be fathers
may be especially common today, when many middle-
class men, married in their teens or early twenties, are
as desperate as their wives in their efforts to conceal
their age. Since paternity is too obvious to be denied,
such fathers often try to mitigate it by playing peer to
their adolescent boys. Even at forty-plus, however,
men may be reluctant to accept the father role. If
children are unruly, unsuccessful at school, inept, or
unpopular, father blames not them but their mother.
Rarely does he assert his authority in order to change
the situation, and when he does, it is often fruitless;
he acts clumsily, self-consciously, because he is not
behaving in the way he prefers. To be the real head of
the family, to act effectively as a father and so offer his
son a model of male behavior different from that of
any of his peer group, say, the father must be an adult,
but too many American fathers resist growing up.

Although some men cherish the appearances of masculinity to the verge of fetishism, although the red-
blooded he-man is the ego ideal glorified by the mass
media, although everything from automobiles to shav-
ing lotion that a man may be expected to buy is marketed with the seal of approval of a broad-shouldered,
slim-waisted athlete whose muscles are evident even
under smoothly fitted evening clothes—in spite of all
this the contemporary American male is apt to be
passive. He does not want to be an adult upon whom
his son can model himself; he is as much in need of
mothering as is his son.

The father's desire to take a back seat in his family
is only one aspect of the passivity which men tend to
show in present-day society. Karl Stern, in his recent
study, *The Flight from Woman*, sees many of the
character disorders encountered among male patients
in terms of their desire to be passive. The patient may

seem busy enough, Stern says. He disdains mere thinking and exacts action as an aim in life. He accepts responsibility. He pursues success. He deals with his
body as if it were a machine with no trade-in value,
to be worn out in work. Often he is referred to psychotherapy by a physician who is treating him for peptic
ulcer. Many of these patients seem anxiously determined to reject dependency; they are afraid to accept
tenderness; they may avoid deep emotional involvement even with their own families and rebuff any attempt at a really affectionate relationship with a
woman, however much they may exercise, and value,
sexual prowess. Yet these very patients reveal that, unconsciously, they have an extraordinary desire to be
mothered; denying that need on an emotional level,
they express it organically: their stomach eats itself
into sores because their emotions, the need for affection and tenderness, are not fed. Another group of
patients live in terror of their desire to be emotionally
dependent, but these patients do not make themselves
sick; they immerse themselves in work, using it as a
means of diverting themselves from accepting love. To
share a genuine love relationship would render them
dependent.

Stern presents an accurate description of many a
present-day father. He is the harried businessman, the
high-strung sales manager, the executive operating
under continuous pressure, the independent professional who rarely lifts his nose from the grindstone.[4]
Even if his position does not actually require such intense concentration on his tasks, he may feel that he
will lose status unless he gives at least the appearance
of devotion to his job.

The desire to hold others at a distance, the apparent
fear of other people's affection indicates the terror of
dependence which moves many men to keep their
emotional relations shallow (and hence comfortably
manageable) and, especially, to refuse the role of

father. For the father is dependent on his children in a
peculiarly intimate and almost painful way. Children
represent his link to past and future, to the community in which he lives and to the flow of time
through separate lives. Fathers may feel themselves
immortal in their children, their sons especially, but
they also see their sons as signs of their own mor-
tality. A man's sons are thus both his rivals and himself; their successes and their failures reflect on him;
his emotional security is bound up in theirs, as their
security grows at least in part out of their relationship
with him. To a man who exists in terror of dependence,
this knowledge, although it may exist far below the
level of consciousness, presents threat as well as
promise. Often, it makes men unable to sustain a
truly meaningful relationship with wife or children.
Fathers fear to accept the responsibility of a genuine
interchange of affection; they repudiate the psychological duty of serving as model for their sons (and their
daughters) by shying away from home and family
and taking "flight into work."

The distrust of intimacy, the dread of dependence,
the refusal to be a father are all interconnected with
one another and with the male's previous relation to
his own mother. As Stern points out, both the male's
passivity and his fear of it reflect his continuing desire
to be fed. That desire may indicate insufficient or
inadequate feeling in the past or fixation at that point
of psychophysical development where the mother-
who-feeds is all important to an infant's survial, be it
girl or boy.

Too frequently, the American male in his relationship to his mother has failed to grow beyond his
reliance on her for food. In part, this may reflect the
mother's use of food as a sign of, or even a substitute
for, genuine affection. A mother who distrusts the
quality of her love may try to soothe her own feeling
of guilt by inordinate attention to the whole feeding

complex: she may stuff her children, she may pay undue attention to their diet, she may subject them to food fads in the name of preserving their health (or increasing their beauty).

Among certain ethnic groups, particularly, where the memory of poverty has outlived actual hunger, the mother continues to give the child the breast long after he has grown a set of teeth: this not in a literal sense, of course, but in making food a symbol of family unity and family affection. Symbolic use of food goes back to earliest times—to the cannibal feast, and the horror it now arouses in most people—which Freud postulates as the origin of human culture. Men have eaten the bodies of their enemies to acquire their strength and their power. Men have eaten the body of their gods. Why then should men not be fed more than bread and meat by the women who rear them?

They used to tell a story on the lower East Side: Joey took the wrong road, his sister was a good girl, his brother became a doctor, but Joey—nobody could keep him straight. His father had a stroke and died the second time they took Joey to prison; his mother lived on in the Forsythe Street tenement: "I can't go away," she told her daughter. "My Joey will come back some day; he's got to find his mamma home."

Joey came home, bleeding, with the cops behind him on the stairs. He knocked at his mother's door. "I know I'm no good," Joey said when she opened it, "but they're after me, Momma, let me in; I've come home to die."

His mother threw the door open. "Yes, my boy," she said, sobbing; "Yes, I know, but first—a little chicken soup."

Not all the stories are as dark as that, but, in contemporary humor, the Jewish mother, pressing "just a little more fish" on a grown son already surfeited, has come to symbolize all the women who refuse to help their sons grow up and who often treat husband and son alike—as children in need of feeding.

The native American mother has focused less sharply on feeding—although she shows a noteworthy, and emotional, concern with giving her family a "well-balanced diet." She is more apt to feed her son social cues than ethnic dainties but her use of food as an instrument of possession, her reluctance to cut the umbilical cord that binds her son to her is no less than that shown by the ethnic mother. Indeed, whatever her background, the mother in the United States has been far more assertive in her dealings with her sons than is common in Europe. The mother's desire to possess and control her children (and daughters do not escape this) has become an essential part of the middle-class American character.

It may seem contradictory to assert that the mobile American, whose ties to family, to community, and to social background are so tenuous, the man who casts home and parents aside so easily, whether he goes away physically or leaves them behind socially and intellectually, should at the same time be so hampered in the effort to cut himself away from his mother. Sometimes, the American male demands mothering from all the women who come into his life. Sometimes he looks for his mother in the woman he marries. Often, the wife-mother refuses to play the part, especially after she has acquired real children to mother. Husbands feel frustrated then; they are dissatisfied with marriage and family. A chronologically adult male still in search of what Jung calls the "good mother," cannot comfortably take on the responsibilities of growing into a genuinely loving adult father, who can maintain a proper intimacy with his children rather than lapse into the pseudo-peer. Such a parent is likely to use his own unresolved needs neurotically: all but seeking revenge for being separated from the mother he hoped to find in his wife, he denies his son the example that would give the boy a chance to achieve a balanced, secure masculinity.

As Stern's work shows, the American father's refusal to accept his traditional place of primacy and authority in the family is closely related to his tendency to work himself into the kinds of stomach and heart disease which are very closely linked with the experience of stress. Why does the American middle-class father in this presumed age of leisure and affluence continue to center his existence around his job; why does he seem quite as submerged in his task as he was in the days of the 72-hour workweek?

Granted that the American middle-class family is costly; rising levels of expenditure do require higher incomes and these are to be won only by working— or by speculation and financial manipulation which are no less productive of worry and stress. Yet even desire for money does not explain the devotion to work which many young executives show. There they can apparently let themselves go, immersing themselves in their organizations or in their professions as they cannot do with their wives and children. Involvement with those whom a man is supposed to love and be loved by poses far more of a threat to the young executive's psychological integrity and his identity than he feels in the grinding struggle of competition for success. Indeed, it is sometimes quite clear in clinical experience that some men can relate to their families only competitively: they become their children's rivals, particularly the rivals of their sons, for their wives' attention and affection.

Again, the man in competition with his children is, in a sense, one of them; he scarcely can be considered a true parent, whatever the biological and legal relationship. Another reason that so many males reject the father's role in the family is to be found in contemporary attitudes toward sex and marriage. Once, sexual needs, if admitted at all by society, were recognized as a regrettable necessity, to be supplied by the cooperation of a special group of women whose degradation did not consist merely in accepting money; it was her willing participation in sex that degraded the prostitute. A worthy woman, so the nineteenth century's expressed major premise ran, wanted to be a mother; she accepted sex as the painful price she must pay to attain her desire.

Currently, American culture seems characterized by a compulsive urge to heterosexuality and an equally compulsive hostility to sex, a hostility largely based on religious sanctions. Thomas Szasz declares that contemporary heterosexuality is often labeled "freedom"; likewise, hatred of sex may wear the mask of "normality." The culture encourages sexual activity; it permits early dating, Szasz notes; it uses sex as a lure for purchasers. Instead of accepting sexuality as a part of human existence to be dealt with as any other human need is dealt with, our culture turns sex into an object of competition. Thus, a man measures himself against other men by making as many conquests as possible (conversely, a woman shows herself to be successful by having many dates, or suitors, or by being talked about as a good sex partner); whether for man or woman, pleasure seems less the motive for sexual activity than desire to count scalps.

Along with a busy and rather joyless heterosexuality, contemporary American culture is characterized by early marriages, even among the middle class. The median age at marriage is now twenty-one for men and about eighteen for women; that is, of all the people who marry in any given year in the United States, half are younger than the ages given. "An unmarried man or woman past thirty," Szasz writes, "must justify his or her single status, as if it were a defect or dereliction of duty. . . . Still more amazing, there are more than 20,000 children fifteen and under who are married. It is a telling commentary on our sexual morality that the concept of teenage marriage is not rejected so strongly as are a host of other sexual practices."[5]

Marriage has always been considered proper for most people. Even when religious celibacy was most highly esteemed, marriage was considered a general obligation, as indeed it was a political and practical necessity: the state needed soldiers and people to work to feed and clothe them, and marriage was the best method known to assure that children would be born and reared. As for individuals—men married to have their physical needs met; women, to have a source of income; both men and women needed and wanted to be parents. As it became possible for men to have the advantages of a household without the need to marry; as women became more and more able to earn their own livings, marriage tended to become a voluntary enterprise. It might be postponed because a young man wanted to see the world, to try himself at half a dozen ways of earning a living, to make a fortune, to build a fine house for his fiancée, or to find a woman worthy of living in the house he had built. Men might put off marrying for sober *or* frivolous reasons. No longer was marriage—particularly in upper-class and intellectual circles—an all but absolute social command.

But by the middle of the twentieth century, the trend reversed itself: even the beatniks, descendants of old Bohemia, were marrying and breeding. Because of the social pressures currently urging people into matrimony, many males marry young less out of a desire to be husbands and fathers than out of a feeling of need to conform. In many professional situations and in numerous large business organizations, marriage is considered the only suitable state for young men who intend to rise: wives and families are stabilizing factors; a married man with children is likely to take his work seriously; he is not apt to run the risk of losing his job and the income that goes with it. Consequently, other things being equal, married men may be preferred to single men for promotion. Often in "marriages of obligation," as one may call them, compulsive heterosexuality may seem the most important reason for entering a particular union. When the first sexual delights have been exhausted, as they can be, his marriage may have little else to offer the man. Yet there is often a by-product; children will have been born because the contemporary marriage of obligation requires a family, and not the one-child family which was acceptable in the 1920's or 1930's, but rather, since many middle-class and lower-middle-class people have been indoctrinated with jargon borrowed from psychoanalysis and psychology, a family of at least three. (In this version of the psychology of the family, three or more children are required to mitigate "sibling rivalry" and its concomitant neurosis.)

People marrying at younger ages means not only larger families but also familes where the children are close together in age. Women can now decide how large their families are to be and many have determined that they will complete their families before they are thirty-five, say. Numbers of young marriages of obligation, and even matches between people of more mature age, endure only because divorce is unacceptable to their religious belief or because divorce is financially troublesome—the man may have to yield too much of his income to his first family to leave him money enough for beginning another. With divorce thus irreligious, uneconomical, or inconvenient, couples find it easier to maintain the marriage. But such a marriage may well endure in enmity, not in goodwill; it may become the center of conflict between fathers and mothers far more interested in acting out their own hostilities and frustrations than in serving as parents. They project onto their children their own thwarted heterosexuality—and a good deal of repressed or unconscious homosexual feeling, too. Sometimes frustration is displaced, although not genuinely dissipated, in a frantic search for cheap excitement and entertainment. Under such circumstances, the father finds it difficult to behave so as to provide a model of adulthood for his son. A young man who feels that he has been forced into marriage and the mold of fatherhood is bound to resist his chains. Sometimes, he breaks the chain by deserting, if he belongs to the lower-income groups; or by divorce, but in that case, he is rather likely to marry again, still feeling that he is not acting wholly of his own will, and therefore still resentful.

Often the young married male assumes a passive attitude, but his passivity seems to be a kind of sulking—as if he were saying to his wife: "You were the one who wanted this marriage and family; it's your job." Or a man may believe he wants a family when, unconsciously, he does not; often he moves away, burying himself in work if he belongs to the middle class, taking refuge in bars and bowling alleys if he is a blue-collar worker. In either case, the growing son at home reminds the father of himself as a free youth, before he got into "the rat race." As the boy grows, the father recalls that freedom with more and more envy, hostility, guilt. The father may try to escape both his resentment and that remembered self of his, by forgetting his own commitment to marriage. His sons are living reminders that he is a self, a self he cannot escape.

Yet the unwilling husband continues trying to leave that self behind by refusing to act as a father. This refusal and the general decline in the position of the father in the American family are illuminated by some of the ideas about the nature of womanhood expressed by anthropologist Margaret Mead and writers George Sand and Simone de Beauvoir.

It has long seemed odd to students and observers

that the very marked physical differences between the sexes should not be accompanied by equally marked—and measurable—psychological differences. Yet when comparative studies are made, statistically clarified and properly discounted for social factors, the differences which do appear rarely are related to anything relevant, such as intelligence or creativity. (It must be admitted that neither intelligence nor creativity is a very clearly defined category.)

In *Male and Female*,[6] Mead develops the idea that conventional Western notions about the male and the female character are not necessarily connected with the physiology of reproduction. She points out that the constant factor is a division of social labor and function between the sexes; in any culture, each sex assumes a distinctive role which is characterized by an associated kind of behavior, physical, social, and emotional. People who fit the sexual roles designated by the culture are designated as normal; persons who do not are often labeled abnormal or odd. Some preliterate cultures recognize human individuality by providing methods by which deviants can assume the social role of the other sex.[7] Roles are everywhere assigned, then, but the content of role behavior and even the characteristic "temperament" embodied in the role may differ.

Among the Melanesian primitives Mead has studied, women of the Mondugamor people take what we should consider a distinctly nonfeminine stance toward life—they are aggressive and, as mothers, they seem singularly unloving; certainly they feed their babies with a kind of brutal casualness that would tend to make any infant grow up a Mondugamor, hostile, belligerent, competent at hunting and war but lacking the graces—even their utensils are stolidly utilitarian. The Arapesh, who live not far from the Mondugamor, are a gentle, nonaggressive, and rather noncreative group whose principal recreation is playing with the lower lip. Here both men and women are passive; the tribe has very little aggression at its command and the individual who is assertive seems abnormal.

Evidently, then, aggressiveness and passivity are not necessarily male and female qualities, respectively, but, rather, the behavior patterns declared appropriate to each sex seem somewhat related to the pattern and character of the entire culture.[8]

Two Frenchwomen, writing some hundred years apart, cast further light on the problem of the relationship between the social role and biological sexuality. George Sand, who refused to accept the female part her society prescribed, wrote to Flaubert that the intellectual and even temperamental differences between the sexes had been overestimated—merely because the biological and physiological differences were so conspicuous. Sand, of course, was attempting to combine both roles in one life. She had been wife, she was mother, artist, and lover. As mother (and she was something less than successful with her daughter certainly), Sand had to care for and educate two children. As artist, she made her way to a reputation as a serious novelist in a literary world dominated by men. It is interesting that Sand created, in novels like *Lelia* and *Indiana,* an influential nineteenth-century literary convention: the misunderstood woman (one who did not accept the orthodox social role). Sand in her sexual life again departed from the assigned female role, refusing to accept male dominance of herself and her children, wooing instead of waiting to be wooed, and often selecting as her lovers men like Musset and Chopin, younger than she, more or less sickly, and hence in need of mothering.[9]

Simone de Beauvoir, living in a France that restricts middle-class women somewhat less than did the France of George Sand's time, approaches the problem from another point of view. Men, says de Beauvoir, regard women as *the other*. They may cry *Vive la différence!*, yet they reject women as beings of equal worth; women are alien creatures. Women may be denigrated or extolled—Schopenhauer's bandy-legged animal sick twelve times a year or Goethe's eternal principle of femininity—but in either case women are alienated, regarded as objects. Looked upon in this way, women lose value[10] and sometimes are even deprived of existence as persons in order that they may be dealt with as examples of Women, that principle in the universe which is other than male.

In the light of what these three women writers tell us, we may better understand the contemporary American man's reluctance to accept fatherhood as essential to his existence as a man. In the United States, the male may be recognizing that certain of the masculine qualities ascribed to him in his social role are not necessarily his as an indivdual.

For centuries, in Western culture at least, fatherhood has been an essential element in the social role of the adult male. Even when a man chose celibacy as a way of life, he was accorded the title of "Father"[11] and recognized as a spiritual parent. Yet in certain cultures, preliterate though they may be, some of the functions which modern society assigns to the father role are performed by others. Thus, the mother's brother rather than the father may take responsibility for feeding mother and children; he may discipline the young and may well be the person with whom the young male will identify himself. Need we assume that because the male formally attached to a given woman has operated as father of the family for centuries, he must continue to do so forever? When the enormous technological and sociological changes that have occurred since 1763 are taken into account,[12] this assumption seems somewhat unrealistic since it fails to distinguish between what, in terms of instinctual drives, is essential in the expression of maleness, and what is culturally imposed.

Social Roles and Modern Masculinity

It is entirely possible that Western society has moved beyond merely incidental changes in the roles of males and females, important as those incidental changes have been in their effects. Obviously, the nature and content of family life have already been materially altered by these changes, but it is not yet known whether these changes constitute a fundamental alteration in the male-female relationship and in the social character of the "normal" members of each sex. Stern alludes to this problem, too, but his concern is in terms of the fate of the Judaeo-Christian scheme of values should the ancient concept of universal polarity as symbolized by the two sexes cease to affect human thinking. Without polarity, to quote Stern, the "unspeakable mystery of the *and*—of God *and* His Creation, of God *and* His People, of Christ *and* the Church—would be conjured away. For Jewish esoteric tradition and Pauline theology teach that Man and Woman share that 'and.' The sexual 'and' is a reflection of the other—all being is nuptial." [18]

The survival of the Judaeo-Christian tradition seems less to the point here than the question of what sort of structure of values and character is likely to emerge after current shifts in sexual roles have been stabilized. American society—the most developed that world technology has yet fashioned—is in transition between traditional versions of the relationship between men and women and a new version of that relationship. Increasingly, one can see a rising rate of change in the conceptions of masculinity, femininity, of the roles of fathers, mothers, parents, single men and women. Many current views of sexuality are outmoded, so out of harmony with present-day needs as often to be harmful to emotional health. Premarital intercourse, adultery, divorce, variation of sexual desire and behavior which are clinically labeled "perversions," male and female homosexuality—all these phenomena are becoming part of the contemporary notion of what people may expect of one another sexually.

Altered ideas of the sexual roles and of sexuality itself affect the position of the American male as father and influence his willingness either to play the traditional role or to accept some new version better adapted to the needs of people in today's world. Obviously, in a society so materially changed on every level—economic, cultural, social, and sexual—the father's place in the family must change, too. His decline from a position of predominance had to occur since he could no longer command wife and children. He had lost the tools and weapons of domineering. Even the prosperous middle-class father could no longer—to use Samuel Butler's phrase—"shake his will" at his grown sons and use the threat of disinheritance to keep them duly subordinate. No longer was it easy for the father to rule the household by control of the purse: his wife was likely to be working—and at a job paying well enough to allow her to support her children without his help. Such a course might not be easy for her; but the wife's ability to earn a living—and the courts' general willingness to treat wives generously in respect to divorce settlements—imposed an outside limit on the male's ability to maintain dominance over his family.

But command and autocratic rule are not necessary for a father to have certain worthwhile qualities and to fulfill some very important functions in the family. The need for a relaxed, spontaneous intimacy between father and son continues to be important for both, however the family structure may change. The father can still care for his son, not in a feverish attempt to show how much of a man he is, by displaying his accomplishments, but rather in an affectionate willing-ness to introduce his son to life in all its details. If the father is to be restored to a meaningful place in the family—granted that he recognizes he has lost this place and desires to regain it—the help of the mother is required. Modern wives seem to have fallen into the habit of negative criticism. They compete for possession of the children rather than take it for granted that their care—and their affection—is to be shared with the father. Competition between parents intensifies pressure in the family. With parents vying for the children's love, it is all but impossible to main-tain the relaxed spontaneity needed for genuine inti-macy, a family relationship that will foster growth by providing affection and understanding. By renewing what seems like a lost intimacy, it will, hopefully, be possible for fathers to preserve desirable elements of the old tradition without involving themselves in the potentially harmful and completely unrealistic attempt to turn back the social clock.

In conclusion, one sees that the reluctance to accept the role of the father and the decline of the father's position in the family are more than the result of social and technological change. The situation also reflects contemporary attitudes toward marriage and sexuality. We may be dealing with a persistent trend, which often is labeled *puritanism*, of hostility to sex. As compared to France and other Continental coun-tries, the United States has always considered sex a problem. It continues to do so, in spite of the impact of psychoanalysis, of the liberating influence of Kin-sey, of the changed position of women, of economic prosperity, and of all the other influences operating to disintegrate nineteenth-century middle-class values. Ever since William Bradford, in his *History of Plym-outh Plantation,* recorded the story of the Pilgrim who was hanged for having had sexual intercourse with one ewe, two cows, a sow, and a turkey—all of which were hanged on the gallows beside him— Americans have been much too occupied with sexual morality. They have rejected any sort of relaxed attitude toward sexuality and have been deeply concerned with seeing that their neighbors behaved properly. Much of this insistence on regulating sexual behavior, whether by law or by mere social pressure, operates as a gigantic cover-up, an effort to hide the fear that any relaxation would cause the person to lose control, and not only sexually. He would indulge in excesses of aggression or, more threatening perhaps, he would permit himself an overflow of tenderness that would run counter to his conception of masculinity.

Americans live in a peculiarly demanding social environment and by an especially exacting creed: All men are equal. No man is asked whence he comes, who his ancestors were; every man is asked what he can do—and he is required to do his utmost. Mobility, opportunity to rise by one's own exertion is a loudly proclaimed and quite sincerely accepted social ideal. Be he Abraham Lincoln or Sammy Davis, Jr., Henry Ford or David Sarnoff, the man who outstrips his fellows to rise from humble beginnings continues to be an American folk hero.

Nevertheless, some people continue to think of themselves as peculiarly entitled to the community's respect. If it is not readily forthcoming, they feel its absence as poignant injury. And they both fear and resent competition from those whom they regard as their inferiors.

Resentment of this kind, springing from irrational sources, accounts for many kinds of political agitation and even for some varieties of American racism. Persons who have newly benefited from mobility, some contemporary historians argue, are particularly likely to feel such resentment. Confronted with pressure from below, they respond to threat with the classic fight-or-flight response. Politically, they may fight by demanding radical change—movement toward a new society or a return to the "good old days." On the other hand, they may flee politics, crying "a pox on all your voting machines." Socially, they may fight by raising barriers against undesirables: restrictive housing covenants, college admission quotas, "exclusive" clubs. Or they may flee by identifying themselves with the threatening social group—there are gentile Jews nowadays as well as "white Negroes."

We may look at the contemporary American male in the light of this interpretation. He confronts a new social situation, the affluence which at least part of our society enjoys. He also confronts a rising social group, educated women whose sexuality has been even further liberated by "the pill." In many instances, he has retreated into passivity: he refuses to live by old-fashioned conventions of masculinity and, especially, he declines the father role.

For the moment, then, let us consider the American male as part of a group resembling middle-class native farmers and small-towners when they confronted an urban population of relatively recent European origin. Men in today's America, like the "old Americans" during the 1920's, feel that they are having an especially difficult time. They were not too long ago in apparently unchallengeable command of their family. Moreover, the very fact of being a male gave them an assured position in the society. This is summed up in the protest of some suffragettes at the turn of the century when women were campaigning for the right to vote: Mrs. Oliver Belmont, wealthy and beautiful leader of both Society and the suffrage movement, is said to have remarked that a ditchdigger, however dirty and ignorant, could vote, only because he was a man, but women were barred, merely because they were women. As women have begun to

earn an independent living, to become educated, to
work in the professions, to vote and hold office, the
security of male superiority has disappeared, as has
his primacy in the family. Mothers, able to earn money
themselves or, at worst, to go on relief rolls, have
begun to show their preference for their children over
their husbands, even in the small way of paying more
attention to feeding the children than to meeting their
husbands' tastes.

To lose a privileged status is as a matter of course
a major source of unrest and disquiet. This discontent
may animate certain political and social movements
whose slogans proclaim: "Let us progress backward
into the past." Too, feelings of lostness, inadequacy,
lack of purpose, the absence of a secure sense of identity and the desire to remain emotionally uninvolved
all color the contemporary problems of the American
male as father. Fathers can no longer play the traditional patriarchal role; their wives would not, as a rule,
endure it and their growing children would probably
laugh them out of countenance. Yet no role has evolved
to replace the traditional one.

For thousands of years, the sociological makeup of
the male personality has been determined, in a very
large measure, by training to become a father. This
has been one of the ways in which a boy could see
himself as an adult. If perpetuating the species is a
prime object of existence, then the social role of
father gives the male a social and psychological
equivalent to the creative nurturing role of the mother. Increasingly, however, fathers are failing to play
the part assigned them. But if that role is progressively
diminished, what is left?

The pseudo-peer which many a present-day father
tries to be is no genuine substitute for the parent;
rather, the effort reflects a situation in which men are
caught because they want a certain status which is to
he had only by marrying and establishing families,

without commitment to marriage and fatherhood. Such men do not want to be fathers, yet they are, in effect, forced to be; they dare not refuse to comply with the demands being made on them. They give token compliance, therefore; they marry, and sometimes divorce and marry again. They beget children and maintain them. Sometimes, these rather unwilling fathers use their breadwinning role as a means of escaping real involvement in the family.

Thus the cycle maintains itself: a son reared in a family where the mother tends to dominate and the father plays an ambiguous role, failing to offer a model of what a male adult should be, marries in order to show himself and the world that he is a man by its standards. But actually, he rejects the responsibility of a caring father and raises sons to perpetuate his failure.

The gratification of the appetites, acquisitiveness or vanity, is too frequently the motive which prompts to activity, and the prevailing ideas are work! work! work! Intellectual or physical labor so directed as to secure a return in dollars and cents, in honors or sensual enjoyment, is apparently, by the great mass of our citizens, alone regarded as a worthy enjoyment for man.

—J. ELLIS
in *The Avoidable Causes
of Disease, Insanity and
Deformity* (1860)

The nineteenth-century American man was a busy builder of bridges and railroads, at work long hours in a materialistic society.

—BARBARA WELTER
in *"The Cult of Womanhood"*

"We have no art," say the Balinese; "we do everything as well as possible."

—MARSHALL MCLUHAN
in *Understanding Media*

CHAPTER V

Home, Work, and Leisure

We might begin this chapter with a question: "Whatever happened to father's chair?"

The disappearance of the large, comfortable chair which was reserved for father's use—if anyone else occupied it, he ceded the chair as soon as father came into the room—symbolizes the change which has occurred in the American home. Father's chair exemplified the position and the identity of the head of the family, and, as important, it gave the other members a sense of who they were and where they belonged.

As we have said more than once, the old days are gone; no realistic person wishes to try to restore them or even desires to have them return. One need only glance at the descriptions of life in the Victorian household as that is portrayed, even if distorted, by Samuel Butler, say, to see how much insensitive domineering, if not outright brutality, went along with the convention of the father's right to rule. Nevertheless, in the process of modifying the father's domination, essential stabilizing elements have been lost, and very little effective effort has been made to replace them. The American male has lost his position in the home— and this is true whether he is father, son, or brother.

Home

In the middle-class suburban family—and it is this group which, by and large, strikes the note for the tune which most of American society will soon be playing—family unity, as shown by joint activity centering in the home, is disappearing. The old motto might be adapted to: Home is where the heart is— if you have a heart. Sometimes it seems that home is where father's heart is not; home is the place he comes to so that he can go somewhere else. After a full day at the office and hours on the commuter train or in his car on the highway, father hurries in, ready to drink his cocktail before dinner and then either to leave his family to absorb himself in the work he has brought home, or to push it aside by settling down before the TV set. He may play cards at a neighbor's or he may pursue a hobby—gardening, carpentry, or the like; he may even do odd chores about the house. Whatever the hobby, father often pursues it alone, not in the company of his sons; often he will mount his stamps or miter his drawer frames in a part of the house carefully separated from the rest of the family. Indeed, at times one wonders whether the father does not choose his hobbies in order to keep his family at a comfortable distance and so avoid too close an involvement with them.

In spite of the optimists who think that TV may bring families closer together by offering their members some common topic of conversation, sitting in front of the screen is another way of being alone though one is in the same room with other people. It seems a significant comment on the character of family life to assume that, without the banalities of TV entertainment (or without the snippets of news or the occasional serious discussions that TV offers), the members of the average American family would have nothing to say to each other. To be sure, conversation may be something of a lost art in the United States. It rarely has flourished as an art in family circles, in any case, but today the kind of easy intimate talk which once did take place, especially between father and son, has often dwindled into meaningless chatter from which both are glad to escape.

This absence of relaxed and meaningful communication in the family, like the gradual fading of the matter-of-fact recognition that father was the family's head, represents more than mere abdication by the male. Many fathers long for, and some even try to maintain, the traditional atmosphere of "home." They have read stories about the family grouped around the fireside, metaphorically speaking, with mother sewing, father reading, perhaps even reading aloud, and sons and daughters occupied with school tasks. They may have enjoyed other types of family recreation which the whole family could share indoors, or they may have looked forward to the day when they would have families of their own, sharing activities which their own childhood had not provided.

These stories are fantasies, of course: few women sew at home any more and most middle-class youngsters have rooms of their own. Perhaps it is unreasonable to ask the present-day family to be more inventive but there is little initiative in devising patterns of activity in which all the family can share meaningfully.

In our technologcal society, the home has experienced encroachment on every level. These encroachments, by and large, have tended either to undermine the male's position in it or to take him outside, both physically and psychologically. The playmate relationship between young brothers, or between brothers and sisters, is beginning to disappear, if only because play has become more organized, centering about the local recreation center, the school, or the Boy Scout troop: play is no longer a casual and spontaneous expression of good spirits and abundant energy. The relationship between brothers in the home, except when they are quite close in age, increasingly loses importance as the peer group fulfills more and more functions for the young, and even for the older, male.

The teenager particularly leads the major part of his life outside the home. More and more that becomes a place where one sleeps and eats, perhaps—although the young male is apt to fill his hollow legs at hamburger stands and sweetshops as often as at home.[1] The really significant part of his life is spent proving himself, seeking to win status in the highly competitive peer group. He plays games with its members, and much of his standing in it depends on how well he plays. If the youngster plays ineptly, he may manage a team or, with the revival of studiousness after Sputnik, he may still win some favor among his peers by succeeding in other activities it approves. His more strictly "social" life is almost completely determined by the peer group. The young male attends the parties it organizes, he gyrates in the dances it makes fashionable; he wears the clothes[2] the peer group considers appropriate; he dates the most popular girls, if he can, and makes do with others if the girl most sought after prefers other youths.

In other words, he lives in a world ruled by other young males; he has little real interest in the activities that occupy adults although, ostensibly, both at school and in his after-school jobs, the adolescent is preparing himself to function in that adult world. Again, this separation between adults and young people in their teens and early twenties is not wholly novel in the United States. American young people have always led an active social life rather separated from that of their elders. Indeed, during much of the nineteenth century the seventeen-to-twenty-three-year-old age group was almost the only one that had leisure enough for parties and the like; once married, men had to concentrate on their jobs and women had to spend even longer working days in kitchen and nursery. In the early 1800's, foreign observers often commented that society in the United States was governed by the young, particularly by the young girl who was seen and heard in American drawing rooms when European girls of her age still kept their eyes modestly on the floor and spoke only when their elders addressed them. The pace of life has long been speedier here than in Europe; young people here have been quicker to mature socially, and this pace has become so rapid since the 1940's that now young people seem to claim adult privileges almost in kindergarten. (Yet, as noted earlier, the same adult society which encourages social precocity also denies teenagers access to some of the traditional opportunities to grow up—notably the opportunity of real work.)

Since the young male thus withdraws himself into the world of the peer group, a world that has little if any room for parents, the members of the family soon feel separated from each other.[3] This feeling, in many instances, initiates the estrangement and alienation which, to so large a degree, have begun to color American family life. Home then becomes, as we said, the place where one pauses in order to get ready to go out; rarely is home a place where minds and hearts meet.

In considerable measure, fathers no longer try to communicate with their sons on any really intimate level. Yet most psychologists would agree that the crucial factor in helping boys acquire and accept adulthood is a close and affectionate relationship with their fathers. Where fathers are strangers in their own homes, sons (and daughters, too) are likely to grow up without someone after whom they can model themselves. They grow up alienated from others, their fathers especially, and from selves which never have had the chance to move toward genuine maturity. Mothers continue trying to maintain the old type of relationship with their sons, perhaps because their more constant presence in the home affords them greater opportunity to get close to their children. The

mother may even ally herself with son against father,
sometimes unconsciously. Nevertheless, her influence,
too, is waning; as soon as the young male realizes
what the peer group has to offer, he has less need for
intimacy with his mother and their communication
tends to break down. She may disapprove of her son's
friends, or she may distrust the nature of his involvement with them and particularly of their domination
over him, but there is little she can do to change the
situation. She cannot exert direct effective discipline
herself, and she can no longer, to any real extent,
seek to support her opinions and her set of values
with the authority of the father, an authority to which
she may, unavailingly, still want to turn.

The father, then, has lost his traditional influence
in the middle-class family. He, as well as his son, is
estranged and uninvolved in his relationships with the
other members of the household. This, too, is less
novel than it seems to some contemporary sociologists.
In contrast with Western Europe, family ties in the
United States have always been somewhat tenuous,
and the father's authority has long been more frequently challenged than it was in Germany, France, or England. Part of the present sense of estrangement is the
outcome of more than a half century of change which
has been occurring in the pattern of family life con-
currently with changes in the position of women.

Personal and social mobility have removed many
of the physical and even emotional constraints which
once kept people bound exclusively to the family and
hindered their branching out into the larger world.
As American society changed after the 1880's, men
experienced that change as a deprivation. Women
struggled to improve their position, and essential to
that improvement was a lessening of male domination.
Since women were at the bottom, as it were, they
had no place to go but up. Men, on the other hand,
had to yield ground; they could no longer confidently

maintain their traditional monopoly of opportunity
and deference. Single women first and then even middle-class wives and mothers no longer considered the
home as their only possible field of activity: women
created new lives of their own. Married women took
jobs outside the home. Even when they turned away
from serious professional careers, as many well-educated women did during the 1950's and 1960's, they
did not restrict their concern to housekeeping and
child-rearing. Again, the move to suburbia, result-
ing in the separation of so many men from the community where they supposedly lived, left such matters
as the operation of the local school system and even
many aspects of local politics to women, although
American women seldom play leading parts in politics,
whether as party leaders, administrators, or legis-
lators.

Too often it has been assumed that the disintegration of traditional patterns of family living exerts its
principal effect on the children. This emphasis ignores
the obvious: the family as a working unit is made up
of parents and children together. Where mothers become involved in community problems or in jobs of
their own, when children are increasingly absorbed
into the peer group, the father is no longer the link
between home and the world beyond. The world outside has ceased to be mysterious and distant. However frightening that world may be, fathers are obviously no better able to cope with many aspects of
it than are mothers—or children themselves. The father's status has been reduced accordingly. No longer
does he feel secure in the family setting. His position
of authority there has been lost. In many instances,
he may be glad to be rid of the burden of that position.
But he pays for that liberation. He continues to seek
a retreat, a shelter from the particular kinds of competition he encounters in business or his profession,
but he can no longer count on finding that refuge in

his home. Children and wife often live in worlds of
their own which they may not want to share with
him; certainly, wives do not generally dedicate themselves to serving his psychological needs although they
may be more than ever aware of those needs.

Work

The American style of life has been formed by the
ethos of work. American society has its roots in a
peculiarly Protestant version of Christianity and that
tradition is immensely involved with work. If we look
at the Scriptural record in which Protestantism is
rooted, we see that, on the surface at least, work is a
consequence of man's fall. Adam did not plow and
weed in Eden. When he and Eve were cast out for
eating the fruit of the Tree of Knowledge, they were
condemned—she to bear children in pain, he to earn
a living by the sweat of his brow.

During the Middle Ages, attitudes toward work
were ambivalent: on the one hand, men had to work
if they were to eat, be clothed and housed, governed,
or protected from invasion or attack. In this light,
work in all its varieties was considered honorable. But
work also bore testimony to Adam's sin; it was a part
of man's punishment. The medieval world constructed
ingenious compromises: some kinds of work—because
they were untainted by usefulness, as Veblen would
say—were not to be regarded as "labor." Other kinds
of effort—the serf's work in the fields, the journey-
man's work with his hands—could not be thus dignified because they were menial. Something of this
ambivalence toward work is seen in the attitude of the
Roman Church, especially of the monastic orders.
Contemplation was the highest good, but men who
intended to engage in meditation and worship were
also required to work, partly for maintenance of the
monastic community and partly for discipline, if not

as punishment at least as a reminder of man's deficiencies. But even necessary work was considered servile; hence most of it was forbidden on the Sabbath and other holy days. Breaches of the command to do no work on such days were common, of course, but the obligation to refrain from work remained in force and cast doubt on its value.

As a money economy began to replace the simpler agricultural society of the early Middle Ages, industry—which always had been a virtue as its contrary had always been considered a deadly sin—grew more and more respectable. The industrious middle class was gaining in power and in social esteem. Members of that class supported many of the movements for religious reforms which spread through Europe even before the Protestant Revolt and most of these movements attacked the clergy, secular and monastic, for being lazy and idle, for failing to perform the work assigned them.

The Protestant Reformers developed the idea of a "calling," of a man's obligation to be industrious, working hard in whatever station he had been born and by such labor serving God more truly than if he spent all his time in prayer, spiritually beneficial though prayer might be. Men could not redeem themselves by work because redemption came only from God, but they could offer evidence that they had been redeemed by devoting themselves to the sobriety of work.

The Puritans, who were peculiarly important in the settlement of the United States, held rigidly to the Protestant concept of the duty to work.[4] Even if the ethos of work had not been sanctioned by religion, of course, it was required by life in a wilderness inhabited only by small groups of relatively primitive Indians, people who lived by hunting and a nomadic kind of agriculture. Unless the settlers intended to adopt the Indian way of life (and some of them did), unremitting labor was necessary.

Even after the first settlements were comfortably established, work continued to be socially necessary. Only if everyone who could work, did work, and constantly, would the society prosper. Since labor was in relatively short supply in comparison with the land and the resources available, even work with one's hands was relatively respectable, certainly much more so than it was in Europe. Idleness among the lower classes incurred legal as well as economic penalties. New England selectmen might fine the parents of a boy who was neither apprenticed to a trade nor busy on his father's land. On the other hand, it was possible for a former shoemaker like Roger Sherman to become a Founding Father; for a former blacksmith, Nathaniel Greene, to become a Revolutionary general; and for Alexander Hamilton, a gifted, hardworking youth of uncertain legitimacy, to win education, high position, admiration and esteem.

During the nineteenth century, work was considered a social duty incumbent on all who were able to perform it. *Work* was defined as effort expended on the farm, in industry, and in business. People involved in government and the professions were also considered to be at work, but the labor of the legislator or lawyer, even of the minister or the physician, was considered most truly entitled to be called work if it made money for the worker or if it at least served some industrial or financial interest. The possession of wealth did not justify a man's not working. The rentier's role enjoyed little social prestige; a young man who lived on an inherited income without seeking to increase it by going into business or practicing a profession was regarded as a mere drone. In Horatio Alger's stories for boys, where the ethos of industry, aggressiveness, and thrift animates what sophisticated people might consider a rather vulgar fairy tale, the

boy hero is always either poor or impoverished, and
the boy villain is either a rich man's son or a youth
who, like Rosswell Crawford in *Ragged Dick* (earliest
and best of the Alger tales) thinks the world owes
him respect (and high wages) because he is a gen-
tleman's son. The truly heroic figure of nineteenth-
century America was the man who was born poor
and made a great fortune by his own effort.

Thus the legend. In fact, most of the great fortunes
of that period came to men like Rockefeller; they,
too, were born into comfort before they made themselves enormously wealthy. Yet those who loved the
legend—and whose purposes were served by it—could
point to true heroes of the economy, men who, like
Andrew Carnegie, rose from poverty to become mil-
lionaires many times over. But whether the masters
of wealth came of comfortable families or poor, they
claimed to have earned their fortunes by hard work,
although often that labor lay in manipulating the
stock market or contriving ways to exploit certain
advantages of control of large-scale enterprises, rather
than in introducing new methods of production or
improving the organization of industrial processes.

However work might be defined, man had been
made for it. And in the United States nearly all men
—certainly all who counted—dedicated themselves to
this duty to a degree that compelled American artists
like Henry James, for example, to leave and live
abroad because the social landscape of the United
States was too level, too uniform to allow one to write
good novels about it. Middle-class people, who in
England would have had leisure for Society, were
preoccupied with business in the United States. Only
the women were free to cultivate their responses to
existence. So much indeed was concern with the
esthetic side of life left to women that even they
eventually protested. They may have been the saviors
of American culture, as Bertrand Russell is said to

have remarked, but some of them became bored with that high mission.

Certainly, when one studies the American movement for the emancipation of women, one cannot help being impressed by the role of work: not only did women demand access to better-paying jobs, but they also wanted to enjoy the moral benefit of being allowed to become wage earners and professional people. Work was a positive good, an opportunity for growth not to be limited to men.

In the nineteenth century, work was more than a burdensome necessity as it gave the male an opportunity for adventure, for finding himself as a person, for making new starts in life. Yet a man could, if he chose, separate himself from the work he did. He might find satisfaction in that work, or, especially if he were a manual laborer, he might not. (For it is particularly during the nineteenth century that many men, artisans and mechanics, most noteworthily, became alienated from their work. They no longer in any real economic sense controlled the kind or quality of the goods they helped make. The product of a shoemaker's labor, for instance, was the wage he received, not the boots he fastened soles to.) But most middle-class men could feel both that their work was indeed their own and that they existed, as men, outside of it.

In the mid-twentieth century, the situation has altered: the laborer is, more than ever, an adjunct to the machine; his relationship to what the machine makes seems increasingly tenuous. Yet, without his work what is he but a number on the unemployment-insurance service's records or an item in the notebook of an investigator for determining whether he is entitled to what we have come to call *poor relief*? But now the middle-class man has often lost his individuality. He, too, is part of what at least tries to ape the machine, a bureaucratic structure which is presumed to operate impersonally.

Even in the formerly independent professions like the law, fewer and fewer men work for themselves. Many of the newer professions—industrial research, engineering, and the like—can, except in quite exceptional circumstances, be practiced only in large corporate enterprises. Management, too, no longer primarily consists of establishing a new enterprise and taking complete responsibility for its success. Rather, management means taking a place in a fixed hierarchy and, while striving competitively for advancement, maintaining loyalty to the organization.

Allegiance of this kind is nothing new: armies, political parties, churches have all required loyalty to themselves as institutions, and Americans have long experience in this practice. The novel element in the contemporary situation is the degree to which business organizations have arrogated to themselves the right to command loyalty from their employees. They presume to examine people who offer themselves for hire, not only for their ability to handle their jobs but also for general suitability of personality. Personnel departments or department superiors even take upon themselves to scrutinize men's behavior off the job, not merely for drinking or gambling, say, but even for "errors" of taste. William H. Whyte, Jr., can (without apparently expecting to arouse indignation at the need for such counsel) tell people how to evade corporate intrusion into their privacy. The litany which Whyte suggests that candidates for jobs repeat to themselves tells us something about the kind of person considered most likely to be acceptable "on the management team." [5]

Today's business manager likes to think of himself as a professional, but he functions as an employee, what the nineteenth century would have called a "hired hand." His psychological makeup must neces-

sarily be different from that which prevailed a couple
of generations ago. Instead of being adventurously
ready to take risks and responsibility, the manager in
a large organization often is apt to be the sort of person who seeks security; he is, at least unconsciously,
dependent, passive, and submissive.[6]

Dependence and passivity are not characteristics
confined to men in large business organizations; the
academic world, too, demands conformity from those
who expect to advance in it. The instructor who
avoids current controversy and contrives to get published in the accepted journals will move up the
academic ladder; the teacher who cannot enter the
publication rat race, who avoids academic fads, and
maintains his own point of view is apt to be passed
over by committees on promotion, or he is invited to
go on to some other institution.

The qualifications required for holding one's ground
in a great business organization, a huge university,
or a government department are the ability to get
on with other people, to be efficient enough to impress
one's superiors but not so efficient as to antagonize
one's fellow workers, to be casual but not slovenly,
active but not pushing. In striving for major success,
a man must be a ruthless competitor while wearing
the face of a good teammate. One works for one's
own individual interest, but one tries to conceal the
effort. One makes oneself known as a man who is
easy to get along with even while one is trying to
undercut rivals. Such a method of operation, indirect
and playing upon one's relationships to other people,
rather than direct and focused on ability to cope with
objects and processes, is traditionally associated with
the feminine social role; it is women who have had to
gain their ends by submissiveness, passivity, and dependence.

Here again, it is possible to see a social cause of
emasculation. The emasculation of the American male

is, as will appear more fully later, not limited to sexual behavior; it is not simply the outcome of a relationship with a castrating mother. Rather, the capacity of the mother *to become* an effectively castrating figure depends upon the existence of larger social pressures working to dampen adventurous approaches to life. If initiative and willingness to take risks are effectively, although indirectly, discouraged by the conditions of advancement in business, those qualities will be discouraged in the man's personal life, too.

It may, of course, be argued that such discouragement itself bears witness to the influence of the castrating mother. Men brought up by more supportive and sustaining women would be less affected by their social environment; they would not so easily lapse into the feminine posture of passivity. Bureaucratic forms of industrialism prevail in Japan, it is noted; conformity is an honored norm there, yet men do not appear psychologically emasculated. In a culture far more closely related to our own, Great Britain's, women are rather more subordinated, eccentricity is cherished, bureaucratic industrialism is of long standing—and, if current fashion is any indication, it is hard to distinguish boy from girl at sight.[7]

Granted that American mothers, long enjoying a more powerful position in the family than other Western women, may have taken on a sufficiently masculine coloration to affect adversely the growth of their sons into manhood. Yet one cannot ignore the part which social change has played and is playing in reinforcing whatever castrating influence American mothers may exert. A man who learns to work "as a member of a team," to remain self-effacing until a favorable moment to display his ability, to avoid "sticking his neck out," to do as most of his peers do, dress as they dress, drink as they drink, amuse himself as they do—a man who has so disciplined himself can hardly stand fast against the temptation to slump into passiv-

ity. A conformist himself, he cannot consistently take
a stand against his children's governing their lives by
the fads and manners of their peers. He may well
avoid deep emotional involvement, for that threatens
both the passivity he finds comfortable and the masculinity which he is not quite sure of.

In today's world, work, instead of contributing to
a man's authority and prestige in his home, has become a factor in his alienation from it. His attempt,
if he makes the attempt, to think of himself as a masterful figure is undercut by need to develop the kind
of personality best suited to succeed in the large organization. His employer's demands on his time and
his devotion take him away from his family. His work,
too often unsatisfying in itself, is hard to translate
into terms which a child can understand. Work in
management, public relations, even scientific research
and development is difficult to bring into the range of
a child's experience. After all, many areas of men's
work can be understood only after some measure of
special training.

Even so, one might say that men who were sufficiently proud of what they were doing—and sufficiently involved with their families—might find ways
to bring the two into communciation. As matters stand,
however, it is so easy to plead the difficulty of the task
that many men find the separation of home and office
a more satisfying way of handling the situation since,
for one thing, each can serve as a means of escape from
the other.

Yet the man who uses his work as a means of escape loses the gratification of showing his family what
he can do. Formerly, male pride developed more from
a man's sharing his work with his family than from
giving them the money he earned for doing it.

To repeat, the kind of alienation from work which
Marx described as affecting the factory worker now
seems to be coloring the life of middle-class man. Fur-

ther, unless ties between home and the adult working world are established when children are young, it is difficult to build the secure relationships which apparently are needed if young people, boys especially, are to situate themselves comfortably in their expected sexual roles. As a result, the male has become an increasingly alienated person. At his job, he is all too often merely a part of an organization, and a dispensable part at that; at home, he finds it increasingly difficult to talk to his family about his work. He is lonely where he should feel in most intimate communication.

Well-paid work outside the home is, furthermore, no longer the monopoly of American men. Women have always worked in the home and, especially since the rise of the factory system, they have worked outside the home as well. But here, as in the rest of Western society, whatever women did was held to be inferior to the deeds of men. Their labor earned them lower wages (even when the jobs were similar if not identical) and the occupations most usual for women conferred small prestige. Rather, working for a living often lessened a woman's status since it showed that she was either attached to no man at all, an admission of sexual and social failure, or belonged to a family that could not provide for her. As women gained greater freedom, however, their working became more acceptable to society and the desirable jobs tended to be less exclusively reserved for men.

Meanwhile, as has been noted, men found work itself less stimulating even though it continued to absorb their time and attention. Donald Meyer, in *The Positive Thinkers*, conveys something of the exhilaration associated with work in nineteenth-century America. The male was in high demand; strong backs, skilled hands, sharp brains all were welcome—periods of economic depression aside. "A remarkable array of new identities, well-defined in terms of capital, skills, energy, role, advancement, presented itself [to men] everywhere." [8] If an individual took a risk and failed, he nearly always had a chance to start over. If the second chance proved no more rewarding than the first, there was always somewhere else to go for a new opportunity.

A man can still leave, of course; Americans are a mobile people, living in a society which continues to be open in certain respects, but society no longer seems to offer the male more stimulus than threat. He finds it far more difficult to draw from his work that kind of support for his sense of masculinity which it once gave him almost as a matter of course. Instead, he may feel insignificant amid the complexities of the organization which employs him, and isolated in a family that has no real appreciation of what he does during his working day.

Such students of society as David Riesman have contended that the whole work ideal is obsolete. Quite aside from automation, it has become so much easier to produce goods that the supply often outruns the capacity of the market; accordingly, thrift is less valuable to contemporary industrial communities than the willingness to buy. Today few men can find psychological support in their work because it does not offer genuinely satisfying goals and purposes. [9] That should be no source of difficulty, it is argued; only those who persistently cling to an outmoded morality are troubled because men work only to earn an income. Given reasonable flexibility, men can find and develop their interests in their leisure time.

Leisure

But one wonders whether leisure actually can give a man the sense of direction and masculinity that his work once gave him. Traditionally, men have used leisure to restore strength and revive flagging energy so that they might fulfil their function in society, what-

ever that function might be. Leisure, in other words,
has been used to make men more fit for work; it was
not considered to be an end in itself. Indeed, one can
argue that, in a society governed by an ethos of work
—as is still nominally the rule in the United States—
leisure cannot be anything but a necessary evil. Yet
one can contend that men may ask that their leisure
provide at least some measure of relaxation, if nothing
else.

Relaxation, however, no longer seems the inevitable
accompaniment of leisure, in part at least because
work and leisure are less sharply differentiated than
they used to be. In *Mass Leisure*, Gregory Stone argues that all distinctions tend to flatten out, if not to
disappear, in today's world. Even during the nineteenth century, phenomena were kept decently separate: a child was a child; a man, a man. There were
weekdays and there were Sundays;[10] there were homes
and there were workplaces; there were gentlemen and
there were workingmen; there was religion and there
was rejection of religion, there were Catholics and
there were Protestants. Above all, there was work and
there was play. Now, Stone writes, night and day are
one and men may work in either. Little boys wear the
long trousers that once marked the grown man; middle-aged men and women refer to themselves as "the
boys" and "the girls" (they have, incidentally, been
doing that ever since the 1890's at least); religion
"embraces science and psychoanalysis" and the sects
walk arm-in-arm; boys and girls go to school together;
women work side by side with men. And, as every
kind of social distance shrinks, "work and play have
spilled over their former bounds and mingle together
in American life."[11]

Stone does not actually mean that work has become
as delightful as play in contemporary America. Rather,
it seems the other way around: play has become as
strenuously organized as work. Anyone who has read

Eric Larrabee's essay on hobbies knows how many varieties of these exist. But do these hobbies really allow the male who engages in them to relax and enjoy a change from work? Do they encourage him to be spontaneous, to have during his leisure time the freedom of choice he cannot have at work? Certainly, the advertisers and the media they pay for bring considerable pressure to bear in channeling a man's free time into ways that will increase their income. Radio, TV, the films all tell him how to relax in ways that will, hopefully, give him pleasure, but primarily they stress the improvement of his status.

If a man wishes to enjoy speed and freedom of movement, he is pushed into tinkering with cars and racing them, often to his destruction. If he wants to see the world, he is urged to travel on budgets, according to plans that provide for everything in advance and require him to do little more for himself than borrow the money to pay the bill; all else is scheduled and regimented; he is told what to see in the places where he is told to go. He may be physically active to the point of weariness while he is actually as passive and submissive during his leisure trip as he ever was at work. He counts the delights of a journey in the number of miles covered or the number of photographs taken rather than in terms of the quality of the experience which he himself has had.

Leisure for the male is often interpreted as another form of activity, different from what work requires only in being unpaid and of no visible use. With the shrinking distance between working time and leisure time, men's play, to the outsider at least, often looks like a mere extension of work although play is something to which the male passively submits rather than something in which he as a whole person participates spontaneously.

Reading and real conversation with others occupy shrinking portions of leisure. People listen a great deal, but not to one another; rather they listen to mechanically reproduced voices coming at them out of a variety of electronic devices; increasingly, it seems that only the professional person listens "live," and although counselor, social worker, and psychotherapist talk back, they do not talk as equals. Have equals anything to give? many people seem to ask. Why exchange thoughts or words with neighbors, friends, or wife and family when the filmed image of the entertainer, or of the professional conversationalists, the participants in panel shows, talk so much better?

The American male is not yet a creature vowed to silence, of course, but he seems less and less inclined to use words to communicate with people in his environment. It has become difficult for him even to find a place where he can relax either in silence or in conversation. His traditional sanctuaries, the shelters from the refining (or rather, confining) influence of women have disappeared or are in process of vanishing. Neither city nor suburb offers him space and quiet for strolling,[12] for casual conversation over beer or cups of coffee. Compare the dismal American neighborhood bar with the British pub or the French bistro. One scarcely wonders that the American male in search of relaxation takes to fishing or the superhighway. But even there he is under pressure, if only to catch a bigger fish than the other men on the hired boat, to outstrip the car which happens to be driving alongside him. Leisure and work make a like demand that he appear the good fellow while he pursues the rewards of the successful competitor.

Wherever the male turns, he sees his old, easy predominance lost. At work he competes with other men and sometimes even with women, albeit business and even professional competition among men is less direct and more subtle than it used to be. At home, where once the man had no equals and therefore no need to struggle for position, the contemporary American father must compete with his children for his wife's attention and with his wife for his children's love. He can let down nowhere. He's under constant strain because, continuously, he is being required to demonstrate that he is really masculine, because maleness *per se* is no longer taken for granted as it once was; that is, although the man still enjoys a position in society and the family merely because he is a man, both his position and his assurance of maleness seem threatened. Americans talk about masculinity; the middle generation (people in their thirties and forties) tries hard to acquire its trappings,[13] yet men feel under constant pressure to prove to themselves and to other people that they actually are males. As a consequence of this pressure, whether he is son or father, whether he is engaged in a strenuous business or is presumably at play, the American male feels alone, unsupported, unsustained, required to live by a pattern of conduct and in a style of life which no longer appears relevant. At work or at home, at leisure or in the midst of effort, boundaries are blurred, guidelines have gone slack, sustaining conventions are dissolved or are in the process of dissolution. Men in their fifties are often uncomfortable as a result, yet most of them can maintain their style. But their younger sons and brothers are beset with sexual and social problems acute enough, and sufficiently prevalent, for the psychotherapist to call them members of a generation in crisis whether he sees them at work or at play, on the job or in the presumed shelter of their homes.

You and your family are alone,
and the only ones you can really count on
for help and support are yourselves.
No one else cares.
                    —MELVIN SEEMAN
                    in "Antidote to Alienation—
                    Learning To Belong"

For some time now, the impression has been
growing upon me that everyone is dead.
                    —WALKER PERCY
                    in *The Moviegoer*

CHAPTER VI

We Are Alone

The unattached male, bachelor or older man separated from family and friends, is not the only male who feels alone. For even when a person enjoys what are considered normally close relationships, he can feel alone. Loneliness, the sense of being walled away from others, is essentially a problem of isolation and alienation, of separation from those one recognizes as one's peers, of the absence of real involvement with one's ostensible intimates, even, in some instances, with oneself.

The Lonely Pioneer

Isolation is a deeply rooted part of the American experience. The earliest settlers were literally isolated, separated from home by thousands of miles of ocean and, more importantly, divided from their own past by the need to earn a living under unfamiliar conditions. The journey into life on the frontier, a journey repeated generation after generation, tended to make isolation a characteristic part of Americans' experience, and it holds an honored place in American folklore—Paul Bunyan moves deeper into the woods than lumbering required; the Daniel Boone of legend leaves any home he makes as soon as he can see the smoke of a neighbor's chimney. Isolation is conspicuous in the earliest noteworthy American fiction: James Fenimore Cooper's *Leatherstocking Tales* describe the hunter, master of the wild forest, splendidly separated

from the vulgarities of life in towns or even on the
frontier of settlement, all but fleeing from the stench
of other white men's presence. In later books—Ham-
lin Garland's novels, for instance—physical isolation
is portrayed not as liberating but as oppressive, part
of an existence dominated by crop failure, mortgage
foreclosures, blows from nature and distant man—all
of it stemming from the frontier farmer's effort to remain within civilization rather than, like Cooper's
Natty Bumppo, to leave it behind.

This condition is no longer very common in contemporary America, seamed as it is by roads and railways,
yet it has helped to shape some kinds of American
character. But isolation today takes on other forms.
The earlier settlers were often concerned, and concerned deeply, with their relationship to God. They
had accepted the Protestant version of the religious
experience, an experience in which the individual
strives to relate himself to God, a relationship that does
not exist for him merely because he has been born into
a church. Like other Protestants, American males
struggled in isolation although they might seek fellowship, that is, the psychological support to be found
in joining with others of like mind. Yet even in the
search for religious fellowship, as Edwin Bowden
points out, a man frequently wanted to be known and
accepted as "an isolated entity." [1] Here again, isolation,
even spiritual isolation, is not felt to be wholly unre-
warding: like the physical isolation of the frontier, the
isolation implicit in the Puritan orientation required
men, as separate individuals, to confront basic experience, alone, stripped of support from tradition,
from affiliation with comforting institutions.

On the political level, the same regard for isolation
appears, paradoxically combined with the habit of
joining with others. "Independence" has been and continues to be a national value: a true American is supposed to be able to stand alone, to seek no favors from

anyone, to make his own way in the world, to vote for
the best man, regardless of the candidate's affiliation
—or his own. Yet Americans are notably ingenious in
setting up political and economic organizations to
which they give thoroughly nonrational allegiance.

To be independent, to maintain a way of life one has
chosen for oneself requires genuine psychological
stamina. Only a person with a secure sense of identity
can choose a style of his own and keep to it, modifying it only as seems suitable to his own needs rather
than changing in response to pressures from the social
environment. This kind of strength is not often to be
found among people who suffer from isolation, who
may desire intimacy, yet fear that acknowledging and
giving way to that desire may erode what they think of
as the integrity of their personality.

Often, suffering from isolation has been made greater
by what may be termed *cultural isolation*. In a mobile
society like that of the United States, in relation to
national wealth, institutions of aesthetic and intellectual life—professional theater and opera, art galleries,
bookshops, cafés, and other centers of companionship
and stimulation—continue to be relatively underdevel-
oped outside certain metropolitan areas[2] or to be quite
unevenly distributed, people with a taste for what has
been classified as "high culture" often feel apart among
their townsmen. An all too familiar figure in American
literature is the young man (or woman) who feels
miserably alone, cut off from understanding because
he lives in a small town where no one but himself
cares for books and ideas. Literature has paid less attention to the person who is the first, or one of the
first, members of a lower-income family to go to college, who through education acquires more cultivated
tastes than his family and old friends, and who experiences not only isolation but even overt hostility.

Antagonism between the generations exists everywhere—Freud tells us all men have been boys who

wanted to kill their fathers—but this division is compounded in the United States because fathers and sons often belong to different cultures. Again, this is not entirely new: the immigrant's child often broke with his father's ways. Fewer immigrants have come to America since the 1920's, but the son with artistic or scholarly aspirations may be as much a puzzle to the successful professional or businessman who is his father as that father was to his own.

Thus, social and cultural isolation blur into alienation. The young-man-becoming-an-artist is a standard figure of the American novel, so familiar as to approach the cliché. Frequently, like Thomas Wolfe, the author describes a hero who feels alienated from community, from family, from himself—and in that he resembles all Americans, according to Wolfe, who see his countrymen as "exiles at home and strangers wherever we go." [3] And J. D. Salinger's *Catcher in the Rye* shows the American adolescent deprived of ties to his existence by uncaring parents, by inadequate friends, by "phony" teachers. The discussion might be extended, citing book upon book with only slight variations on the theme. Essentially that person would be a male who knows himself to be alone in a world not of his making, who does not want to be alone, and yet who cannot find, either in others nor in himself, the trust which would allow him to develop genuine bonds and true intimacies.

To develop such trust so that he can grow in interaction with others and thus learn to know and to be himself is most difficult for the American male. His first duty is to succeed—to play better baseball, to get higher grades, to date the most desirable girl, to win the best job. That "bitch goddess," Success, is the fruit of competition and however the techniques of competition may change when the game is "for keeps," competitors are enemies. We have seen how, even in the context of the family, sons and fathers may be competitors—and even mothers may be seen less as protectors than as driving forces.

American men, whatever their age, have little time for the contemplation needed to discover the self and few opportunities to be that self if they should find it. Knowingly or unwittingly, they have a sense of being entangled in a web of demands and activities that chokes trust. He tends to feel alone, therefore; surrounded though he may be by his peers and his family, the American male often thinks of himself as isolated in the midst of people who appear neither to understand his need for real human involvement nor to care whether that need is satisfied.

Looking at the adolescent male, one is impelled to question, though one cannot even pretend to offer answers. Do elements of frontier isolation linger in today's world and affect American youths? What has half a century of immigration from eastern and southern Europe done to alter long-standing American family patterns? What, particularly, has been the impact of the affluence which is said to have flooded the country since World War II? Has the contemporary uninvolved style of life relieved young men of their growing pains? Do they, having given up the attempt to establish identities of their own, contentedly accept the substitutes which the mass media offer and so no longer experience the identity crisis which affects so many other people in the society?

Lonely Youth

For young American males to feel lonely and isolated may seem a paradox. Such feelings belong to persons given to thought and brooding rather than to people as immersed in activity as are young men in the United States. Rarely have so many youths had the opportunity to do so many different kinds of pleasurable things: sports, driving, parties—the middle-class young man appears always to be going somewhere. He may be harassed by parents and school authorities and the need to study harder than used to be necessary for admission to a good college, but many a youth is contented with nonprestige schools. Many more young men do not aspire to higher education and the economic rewards it is supposed to bring than formerly. The middle-class teenager looks free, free as no other male in American society is likely to be. To the outsider the years which young men spend in high school and in college look to be a long vacation before entering the real business of adult life.

We have pointed out that this external view is superficial and misleading: the young male is not that free, not that exempt from responsibility, not that joyous. He is indulged; he is even imitated; but he is also exiled, assigned to a subculture of his own. Within the limits of that air-conditioned ghetto, he may be permitted a kind of creativity: he hatches fads, a language, sets of mannerisms. The mass media are quick to report these. On occasion, adults intent on showing how they have preserved their own youth may take up fads and fashion designed for the adolescent and so swell markets and the incentive to create markets. Above all, the adolescent male seems given over to the domination of the peer group—and this is as true of street-corner society as it is of the middle-class world. Youths do not experience isolation so much as the fear of isolation, of being so different from their peers that they will be left out, unpopular, ignored.

The young male experiences another kind of separation, however, and this is a consequence of the breakdown of communication between adolescents and the adult world, especially as that world is represented by parents who, pathetically, seem to want to put themselves on a level with their sons. As one teenage boy is quoted: "Adults are their own worst enemy. I mean, my dad's trying to learn the twist and all. They try too hard and they do it all the wrong way. They'll read a book on teen psychology, and that's no good. *There's no real talk between kids and adults.* [Author's italics.] I mean, whoever talks to their parents about sex anymore?" [4]

The fear of being alone is associated, in the young male, with a pervasive boredom. For all the variety of diversions available, customary activities seem to be losing some of their charm.[5] The poet Gregory Corso, talking to a group of Buffalo teenagers, found them agreeing with the college freshman[6] who declared that high-school seniors lacked direction. What they wanted to do, where they wanted to go, they did not know, "but they feel that they must always be on the move. . . . They must never sit home and relax." [7]

This inability to relax at home colors the whole situation of the young man who lives in fear of loneliness. The lack of intimate ties with his family almost compels him into constant movement. Again, one may ask is this alienation from their presumed "nearest and dearest" the rule? It seems possible to say yes—without, of course, denying the continued existence of old-fashioned families in which parents and children do maintain a relaxed intimacy with each other. The intense pressure of today's urbanization seems to be pushing against these islands of genuine family life. As that pressure increases, as more and more areas are drawn into the "urban sprawl" which is so rapidly overwhelming the rich, self-contained entity which constituted a city in the nineteenth and early twentieth centuries, the closeness of family life is likely to be further eaten away. With the dwindling of that intimacy, the teenage male is likely to feel more alone than ever.

Furthermore, the time between generations is speeding up. Once we counted thirty years to a generation, then twenty; now the time seems to have shortened still more. Such an acceleration exerts a great threat to the young male's security, caught as he is between a family where there is little intimacy to afford him psychological support, and a society which demands that he keep "on the move," wanting more and more things, shifting from one peer group to another so that he may rise in the world. A young man bound into such a social pattern finds it hard to establish the kinds of tie that will buttress him against fear of being alone. Really close relationships with other young males have become increasingly difficult, partly because nonplayful competitiveness begins rather earlier than it used to, partly because a pseudo-sophistication and too little knowledge of psychology cast suspicion upon such relationships as being homosexual. Genuine intimacy with young girls is even more difficult: friendships which express themselves in sexual relations have emotional as well as biological consequences. Early marriage, often chosen as a kind of insurance against loneliness, frequently proves disappointing: the familial pattern of alienation is reproduced with the birth of children.

The young man may find ways other than marriage to ward off loneliness. Juvenile delinquency among middle-class youngsters seems to be a response to boredom and lack of direction, as in the lower-income groups delinquency appears to result from lack of opportunity—and from boredom.[8] Excessive drinking may become a problem on both social levels and many college-age youths are experimenting with hallucinogenic drugs.[9] Young males have been smoking marijuana for a number of years now; the habit has given rise to much argument: Is marijuana truly addictive; is it likely to lead its users to more definitely addictive narcotics? Marijuana is being supplemented, or perhaps supplanted in a fashion, by mescaline (the effective chemical constituent of peyote) or even more so today by LSD. The appeal which these drugs have[10] attests to a kind of boredom which has transcended

mere ennui and become despair. The customary stim-
uli—speed, sex, violent activity, even delinquency—no
longer provide the desired "kick." For many people,
the "consciousness-expanding" drugs seem to gratify
the need for intense experience without effort. LSD
and the like provide vivid fantasies, while the person
himself remains *passive*.[11]

The teenager often fears being alone, then, and he
flees from his fear into peer-group activity, what is
jeeringly referred to as "instant Nirvana," or into marriage that resembles a game of fantasy, especially if
he belongs to the reasonably prosperous middle class
and has some confidence that his parents, however distant emotionally, will act to get him out of difficulties,
will even, if necessary, help pay for a divorce.

Thirty-plus and Lonely

Youths under twenty may fear they will be alone,
but the man who does not marry soon after he leaves
college, or the man who stays single after the middle
thirties is apt to be alone. Some older unmarried men
have been either widowed or divorced; often, they are
in their sixties or beyond and their loneliness is compounded by want—they are the people who figure in
the statistics of poverty, men who have been "retired"
to the social scrap heap where they are expected
quietly to wait for death.

The common fate of these people must give a dark
tinge to the loneliness which many younger single men
experience. What, in fact, does being single mean for
the male in contemporary American society? He seems
to function principally as quarry, an object to be
hunted by women in search of mates. As Shaw says of
Shakespeare's plots, "the interest is the interest of seeing the woman hunt." Later he describes the social
struggle between the sexes: "It is a woman's business

to get married as soon as possible, and a man's to keep unmarried as long as he can."

Contemporary American society tends to find fault with the man who succeeds in avoiding marriage. Single women are less harassed: they cannot be blamed for being single since, presumably, they must stand by until some man asks them to marry. If they have not been asked, they may be looked down upon as being incompetent in the art of maneuver, or as being insufficiently attractive to win a husband, but they are not considered to be wilfully refusing their social duty.

The bachelor may be a more welcome dinner guest than the spinster, but his bachelorhood is regarded with disfavor rather than with the contemptuous pity which the spinster still encounters. It is assumed that a man ought to marry, certainly by the time he has reached thirty. If he has not by then, and if he chooses to remain single thereafter, he has shirked his social responsibilities.

If one agrees with Thomas Szasz that our society is compulsively heterosexual, then any unmarried male over thirty will appear suspect, labeled sexually inadequate, neurotic, or homosexual. The bachelor was once as readily accepted in the United States as he continues to be in Europe; Americans, too, welcomed the single man as a friend of the family. But nowadays a single man in that role would be speculated about: Is he the wife's boyfriend or the husband's; has he a peculiar and suspicious taste for little children; or is his presence innocent after all, with the husband's or wife's sister as the reason for his visits? Even within his own family, the single male over thirty may feel somewhat less than accepted. His mother may enjoy having him about, especially if she is a dominating person, but he has no recognized function anywhere else in the family. The wise, kindly bachelor uncle used to be an important figure in the lives of his brothers' and sisters' children; he was the source of treats and trips, of wonderful stories, even of the young male's initiation into the world of club and tavern, of the theater, prudent gaming, and a little judicious wenching. "Uncle Max" was as reliable as father was, but he was amusing and full of surprises besides, unlike many fathers. Part of the bachelor uncle's charm was command of an income which did not need to be shared with a family; thus he could give his nephews and nieces small luxuries, even, sometimes, providing real assistance.

So it used to be. However, the single man no longer has an accepted place in contemporary America. He must defend himself for remaining unmarried; often he is all but required to prove that he is not a homosexual. Overwhelmed by the pressures of a society that frowns on bachelorhood, some bachelors yield and marry, in self-defense and against their true inclinations. Certainly, the single man is under constant pursuit by hopeful women. When he does make women friends who accept his intention to remain single and to avoid any permanent sexual involvement, he is likely to find that these friendships present him with a whole set of problems. In a society apparently bent on thrusting as many people as possible into marriage, a woman in her thirties who has failed to acquire a husband (or has chosen to remain unmarried) is something of a social anomaly. She is patronized rather than blamed, perhaps, but her status is not enviable: socially, she is apt to be herded with other women; at work, her life is apt to be an all-feminine affair in the office clerical workers' pool, or at school, library, and the like. All too frequently, the mature single woman turns her men friends into psychological confidants, a role which few of them welcome or are competent to undertake.

The single man is likely to be even less physically and socially comfortable than the single woman. Many men have developed housekeeping skills, but that is not entirely approved (although it is fashionable for men to cook elaborately). The old-fashioned boarding-house—which had little to recommend it at best—has disappeared. Agreeable social gathering places are not readily available to the middle-class bachelor. The pub so characteristic of English cities and towns is infrequently found in the United States. The single man alone in a large city, where close friendship with other men is frowned on, where married friends constantly thrust women at him, or where he may have no friends at all, is doomed to rather a cheerless life.

As the single man ages, his position becomes even less enviable. The heterosexual world has little if any room for him, yet he may not be at all homosexual. Thus the single male may come to feel himself an ex-ile from both worlds and ultimately, like the teenager frightened of being alone, he may marry or he may simply continue to bear the weight of alienation and to experience the full burden of loneliness.[12]

Alone in the Family's Bosom

Most people in our society do marry as expected, however; and we have noted that many youths turn to matrimony as a sort of insurance against being alone. The young man who, according to convention, marries sensibly a woman of approximately his own age and social status, who earns enough to keep her and their young children until she can return to work, if necessary, seems to have all that may be re-quired for a secure and comfortable life: a job to keep him alert and busy during the day, and a pleasant suburban home to return to later, well equipped with electronic aids to housekeeping and to pleasure. Yet from the material in books like Whyte's *The Organiza-tion Man,* Seeley's studies of suburbia, Keats' on the crack in the picture window,[13] and in a whole spate of articles in magazines and professional journals, one

can see that even prosperous communities have their
share of loneliness, of separateness.[14]

Often, suburban isolation is described from the
woman's point of view. It is the college woman especially who, in spite of recent studies which show the
contrary, is seen, and sometimes sees herself, trapped
in suburban housewifery. But the young husband, too,
may feel trapped: physically, because of the time he
must give to longer and longer journeys between home
and work; financially, bcause he must earn money
needed to sustain a young family; psychologically,
because he is bound to routine and enveloped in
ennui.

The young married man may enjoy a high standard
of living in terms of possessions,[15] but maintaining a
large enough income to meet payments on mortgages
and other installment debts gives him little chance for
the spontaneity and innovation that would enrich his
existence. He may seek a new job, of course, but he
does not often feel ready to risk his income in order to
turn to a new profession. Even an affluent young man,
successful and apparently well-adjusted, may sometimes wonder whether his electrically operated Eden
really compensates for the barren routine to which
so much of his life is reduced.

The psychoanalyst may well see The Organization
playing something like the father's role in the young
married man's life, while his wife serves as some
aspect of his mother. Yet he can establish no real
intimacy with these pseudo-parents either. He may
attempt to protect himself from feeling the emptiness
of his relationships by trying to exist in cool detachment from his life. But detachment is merely defensive;
it cannot confer freedom and care.

In patients who have developed this variety of
detachment, the psychotherapist encounters a kind
of muted apathy. Wherever such a patient turns, he
finds a disappointment. Work offers some stimulation,

of course, but its rewards are often not satisfying. Marriage fails to provide the anticipated safeguard against loneliness. Alternatives to marriage are no less disappointing. The understanding woman who is content to be an undemanding mistress is a mere figment of male fantasy. Divorce may mean only further entrapment: payments for the support of wife and children leave only a portion of the male's income free for a new life; his second family must either live less well than his status would warrant, or he and his new wife must work harder than ever.

Prime and Decline

If the younger married man has not won security against loneliness, the position of the mature male is little better. Curiously, as the life span lengthens, men are considered old at a younger age. Some decades ago, men began to worry about aging at fifty; now they worry at forty. Since the 1920's, both blue-collar and white-collar workers have found it hard to get jobs if they were over forty; now executives in middle management and even persons on higher levels of the organizational hierarchy are concerned lest, if they are not successfully placed at forty, they will move only down the ladder. Even shifting from organization to organization seems to present hazards for those who have not advanced close to the top by their early forties.

The American male in the prime of life, therefore, stands in a peculiar situation. In earlier decades, men of that age were usually heads of a family of adolescents; now they may well be grandparents because of today's early marriages. The male who is a grandfather at fifty is indeed biologically unnecessary; his essential function in the world has been filled. In modern society, the man of fifty may have even passed the peak of his earning power unless he is one of the extraordinary few with the capacity to achieve a really dominating position. Certainly, he experiences the competition of younger men as a real threat, and this the more especially as the first offspring of the "baby boom" of the late 1940's begin to clamor at the gate. Only in the political world does maturity continue to seem relevant: the elder statesman holds his ground—certainly de Gaulle and Adenauer have shown themselves competent to get and hold power and, occasionally, to perform as genuine statesmen.

The married man in his fifties, with the prospect of an early retirement—what has he to anticipate? The wife to whom he might have looked to protect them both against the feeling of being alone—and superfluous—is herself deeply involved in the struggle to stay young. Early marriage and early motherhood make her particularly determined to retain her attractiveness. Often, in the family, she becomes her daughter's rival for her husband's attention. Which of the two will he prefer? Frequently, the father does not wish to make the choice and, as frequently, the daughter's early marriage makes that choice unnecessary. Yet even after that problem is resolved, the father cannot face retirement with the assurance that he will not be alone. His children, if current patterns of early marriage continue, will have set up homes of their own and at some distance from the parents. His relation with his wife is apt not to be deeply gratifying on the level of companionship. His friendships are pleasant but superficial: he has changed peer groups as his parents moved; shifting from job to job and place to place, as he is likely to have done, has hindered his forming enduring relationships—even if society did not show its suspicion of deep friendships among men. Thus, when the older man no longer has his work to provide contacts with people, and the tenuous bonds that may develop from them, he is more alone than ever.

Small wonder that separation from the job so often operates as a death sentence. The habits fostered by the strain of competition in the contemporary world do foster deterioration of the body. The character structure of the other-directed man, who seems best adapted to success in large organizations, does not tend to help a man develop inner strength. Hence, once deprived of the work which is his immediate reason for existence, the male may experience severe depression or other signs of emotional breakdown. Retirement, however comfortable, may be merely the prelude to death.

Industrial societies have long been characterized by the loneliness and isolation which a man is apt to experience. He has traditionally borne the brunt of earning a living for a family in a competitive world which required him to work at jobs that were not psychologically rewarding. In compensation, the male was accorded a favored position in the family whether he was son, brother, husband, or father. All men were superior to all women. Whatever his class, the male as male had prestige. However small his income, however low his status, the male usually had women and children to lord over.

Rarely did being alone in the world appear to be one of the hazards of the middle-class male's existence. Men might be forced into loneliness, of course, but they were the derelicts, the ne'er-do-wells, the incompetent, the delinquent; the prosperous confidently expected personal and family relationships to keep a man from being alone. Even the bachelor had a place because he had friends and family to fall back on.

Industrialism, with its disintegrational impact on family life, has made home and family less and less certain a refuge against isolation and alienation. As the most unadulteratedly organizational society, the

United States has seen the escape hatches close earlier
than Europe has. Hence, it is in America that the
male seems most in fear of being alone. He encounters
the result of trends long operative in the society, but
which now appear to have reached their culmination.
Contemporary loneliness is associated with crowding
—even in the new suburbs and the more spacious ex-
urbs, people are forced into close quarters. What
emerges are friendly but casual relationships that
avoid deep involvement, even with those who suffer
greatly from being alone. This condition is intensified
by our self-consciousness; in an odd way, people are
aware of what is happening to them even though they
apparently feel helpless to do anything about it.[16]

In today's world, it is the male who meets the impact of change most immediately. He is the person
first required to adapt to the needs of today's marketing phase of industrialism. Changes in the position
of women make them less useful shields for a threatened male ego. But that ego is also attacked directly.
It is hard for contemporary man to develop a sense of
his identity as a man, both because he lacks models
and because so many of the traditional male roles
are either wholly obsolete or have so changed that
they are less supportive. Soldiers, for example, meet
less and less often as equals in combat. Mechanized
warfare sometimes seems to make the fighter as much
an accessory to his machines as the industrial worker.
Business, however much it requires a man to be an
effective competitor, has so changed the pattern of
competition that it no longer encourages pronounced
initiative and self-confidence. Fathers no longer rule
exclusively or exclusively provide for their families.

The male feels alone wherever he turns. The traditional protections have lost their effectiveness; new
kinds of protection have not yet made their appearance. Perhaps, in a few decades—since all aspects of
existence accelerate—a new kind of character struc-

Unusual conduct isn't necessarily neurotic.
    —SIGMUND FREUD
    in Joseph Wortis'
    Fragments of an Analysis with Freud

The Victorian nice man or woman was guilty if
he or she did perform sexually; now we are guilty
if we don't.

        —ROLLO MAY
        in "What Is Our Problem?"

All our problems concerning sexuality seem
to have come from the collapse of an ancient
understanding of the sacred which gave almost
total meaning to human sexuality. The ethic
of modern marriage is one of the relatively
successful responses to this collapse.

        —PAUL RICOEUR
        in "Wonder, Eroticism,
        and Enigma"

CHAPTER VII

The Emasculation
of the American Male:
Aspects of Sexuality

Ours is a culture in which at least nominally the masculine element is dominant. The language itself bears witness to this, for it says "man" when it means the whole body of human beings. In the continuing colloquy about sex roles which sociologists and psychoanalysts have been carrying on, the primacy of the male is at least tacitly assumed, since most writers deal with the problems of women who can no longer live easily and comfortably in ways which foster the feminine attitude—passive and receptive in contrast to the active and aggressive posture proper to the male.[1]

Nevertheless, it has become increasingly evident that the contemporary situation presents so many barriers to the assumption of the traditional masculine stance that one may speak of the emasculation of the American male. Many discussions of the role of today's women use the psychoanalytic concept of penis envy as the key to understanding their problems: all little girls believe that they too once had a penis, but have lost that symbol of bliss. Many little girls, *chronologically adult*, lead lives which are a search for something lost which they never had. Conversely, all girls, and in America, many little boys, *chronologically adult*, live in ways that show they fear to lose, symbolically at least, what apparently they still possess.

This statement is neither vulgarized psychoanalysis nor sociological hyperbole; it states the psychotherapist's clinical experience with many patients. Analysts see more and more men who feel that they are inadequate in a way that goes beyond a sense of ineffectiveness in daily life or even of sexual dissatisfaction. Evidently such feelings of inadequacy are rooted in the personality structure of contemporary American man. One then raises the question: what is responsible for that peculiar personality structure?

Dwindling Status

It is currently fashionable to answer, the American woman, especially the aggressive American mother. But women and mothers do not function in a social vacuum. The American male is involved in a status revolution not unlike that which occurred during the nineteenth century in the United States when the older dominant social group made up of professional men and persons who had accumulated a competence in commerce or small-scale industry saw their fortunes and themselves dwarfed by huge fortunes concentrated in the hands of new men who held unprecedented economic power. Today's sociological developments, particularly the contradictions which characterize our affluent society, have made it easier for women to express aggressiveness, but the American mothers' dominant role in the family began in the early days of the American experience. A European middle-class mother could be held to decorative and housekeeping functions in the eighteenth and nineteenth centuries. A European lower-class mother was rather generaly expected to accept and even to enjoy, an occasional beating from her husband. Neither had much chance to direct her own life; neither had a determining role in making family decisions. Unless she were especially gifted, especially pretty, especially enterprising, or especially religious, the European woman moved out from under her father's thumb only to find herself under the thumb of her husband —if she were lucky enough to marry, since men were scarce, particularly men of suitable social position.

This situation was less true in the United States, although here, too, men, at least in theory, governed the family as well as the state. During the formative years of settlement and national growth, women were necessary in the household if men were to enjoy the simple comforts of warm meals and mended clothes, to say nothing of sex and sociability. In the struggle for a civilized existence, the American wife played a more crucial role than did her counterpart in Europe, where civilization and the life of the mind had long since matured—and matured as a primarily male concern. Among nineteenth-century European migrants, men outnumbered women; the wife and mother thus acquired a new importance; she was more necessary than she had been, even in a peasant economy; and in spite of economic burdens and language barriers she learned that both among the ruling native groups and among immigrants of long tenure, a woman was treated with greater regard than she had been accustomed to. Later, as industry and business grew, American middle-class women found new opportunities for work outside the home, and this ability to support themselves tended to strengthen their domestic position. Greater access to money and to education, added to the customary respect accorded American women, led them to become more demanding. At the same time, American men left them more of the responsibility for ruling the family and maintaining the nation's cultural life.

Trends long evident have risen to a climax in our time. The mores continue to demand what they have long demanded, that men be men, aggressive, competitive, successful. The most valued success remains, as it has been, economic. The struggle for that kind of success continues to separate men from home and family; it has been and still is carried on at a high level of tension, leaving the successful man with little energy to run his family, which seems less important than running his business or holding his job. Successful men left their families to their wives because they had better things to do. Unsuccessful men found it difficult to assert themselves at home because their lack of success, so highly visible in a society which measured worth by earning power, deprived them of confidence and even of domestic prestige.

Consequently, for a number of generations, American men have not only been fostered and cherished by their mothers, they have been instructed, guided, and disciplined by them. Father might be masterful at the office, efficient to the point of ruthlessness; he might be a thorough "he-man" scornful not only of art, letters, and learning, but even of politeness. His strength and effectiveness were exerted out of sight, however; it was mother who was there. Or, if mother were absent, teacher was there, equally in command, equally a woman.

Thus, long before mid-twentieth century, when the problem began to attract attention, the American boy was beginning to derive his model of authority from his mother. Fathers provided decreasingly useful models of potency and maleness. Being a man continued to be desirable and boys aspired to become men— heroes of the Great Outdoors, heroes of the ball field, the financial markets, the boxing arena—they aspired to make great fortunes or earn high wages. But few boys thought of being a father as one of the rewards of growing up. As described earlier, the role of father was truncated: father as provider, yes; father as authority and educator, no; father as a kind of pseudo-peer, maybe, but always uneasily—the peer is, after all, a rival.

The mobile technological society which is so characteristically American provides psychological support for man-the-economic-competitor, but it does little to bolster men-in-the-family (if we may use an existential turn of phrase). Rather, a changing society brings new pressures to bear against those feelings of adequacy which are difficult enough for the boy to establish. The psychoanalytic picture of his development shows that the boy must forego jealous hatred of the mother-possessing father sufficiently to establish the kind of identification which will enable him to grow into a man and the ability to become a father himself. If the father appears strong, competent, kindly, and wise, as well as successful in the struggle for the mother, the boy's identification with him may become easier. Of course, it might be argued that the contemporary American father with his diminished role in the family is the traditional father, just because he is less evidently in possession of the mother and less dominating in the household. For this very reason, however, because the father does seem more the son's equal, his privileges, though restricted, appear the more irritating. Envy is said to be the peculiar vice of democracy: where all are supposedly equal, superiority galls more harshly than it does in a situation where men take their places assigned them in a time-honored structure. Similarly, in the modern "democratic" family, father's few remaining privileges are offensive to the son who has been brought up to believe there should be no privileges at all.

In a social context which allows a young person to know what is expected of him, the boy can make the necessary shifts in attitude with a minimum of shock and suffering. Difficult though the boy might find it to alter his feelings about his father, he could nonetheless find assurance in his own masculinity. During the nineteenth century and down through the 1920's, perhaps, that assurance was not much disturbed. The American man might experience some doubt about his

position as head of the family, but he was safe as far
as sexual performance was concerned: whether he
bought milk as needed or invested in a cow, satisfying
women sexually was no problem of his.[2] Prostitutes
deserved no consideration and wives required none:
by definition, the middle-class wife was a nice woman, and nice women (like their male counterparts)
thought sex too dirty to be a source of satisfaction
(or at least were supposed to think in that way).

Thus, so long as the values of traditional society
continued to dominate, the American man enjoyed a
degree of security as a sexual being, however dis-
turbing his society might be. But following upon
World War I society and women alike began to make
new demands upon him. A growing economy created
new jobs and careers, but these did not help him
establish a sense of continuity as male-in-command.
Technological and socioeconomic changes, as has been
pointed out, separated the male even further from his
family. He was increasingly removed from familiar
environments, from the supervision of old friends and
neighbors, even from the peculiar and possibly stable
value systems of the lower-income ethnic group out of
which he must move if he was to experience any real
economic success.

Women, however, found their change of position
no less cataclysmic. They, too, had new economic opportunities. Industrial society had made the home
obsolete as a center of production, but the development of trade and finance created a large demand for
women workers just at the time that the growth of an
economy of consumer durables and a processed-food
industry made them less useful in the home. Yet
women encountered certain attacks on their security
along with their new chances for independence.
As divorce became more socially acceptable, for instance, the middle-class woman could no longer regard
her husband as a lifetime possession; she could not

take her marriage for granted as a permanent arrangement. Emancipation had its costs for her. But few of the women concerned with enlarging their own opportunities considered the effects which their altered position might have upon the male.

Initially, many women expected to choose between careers and marriage; they did not assume they would have both. Today, middle-class women often must base their lives on the knowledge that their earnings are necessary to give their families a suitable living. They do not choose between jobs and marriage but assume that their wages are needed to support the marriage. This has had a somewhat castrating effect upon the male. In an already highly competitive society, men receive further competition from women, especially in the lower segment of white-collar employment and in the less highly regarded professions, such as college and university teaching. Secondly, the economic emancipation of women has deprived men of even a token presumptive right to dominance in the family. There men today must struggle to hold even an equal position against the competition of a rather better-equipped rival. In male-dominated societies, women have had to learn the art of manipulating their masters in order to survive as individuals. But American men often have seen themselves pushed into a secondary position vis-à-vis children and wives. Biologically, this may be wholesome, and of course, in the long view of the survival of the species, "women and children first" may have some validity, but men are accustomed to lead. And the American male who has brought competitive free enterprise to so high a level of effectiveness has proved much less effective in competing within his own family.

Frequently, he has tended to retreat from the family into business or into the all-male group where competition proceeded according to rules with which he was familiar. The growth of organizations like the

Lions, Rotary, the Elks, and even the Masons indicates how the male, in the nineteenth and early
twentieth centuries, fled from the increasingly child-
oriented and woman-ruled home to the more congenial male group. Women intruded even here, however—Freemasonry, for example, which continues to
be upper class in many European countries, has become increasingly middle-class in the United States,
and even includes a ladies' auxiliary, as do the other
fraternal orders. Since the 1930's, American business-
men's luncheon clubs and fraternal societies have
lost social prestige; the "secret" orders have begun
to lose middle-class membership in larger communities. Much so-called club life in America is carried on
for the purpose of business; little of it resembles the
English men's club, which provides a genuine alternative to home and family. American men may wish
to turn aside from domesticity and enjoy the freedom
of the socially approved all-male group, yet, as has
been remarked earlier, it is increasingly difficult for
them to do so.

Even when the male does achieve some degree of
"liberation" from the wives and children who so often
make him feel like a weekend guest in his own home,
he appears to be an isolated and estranged being. All
the noisy joviality of "good fellows together" cannot
create genuine camaraderie, cannot conceal the individual's real fear of being left out, alone. Men
appear somewhat less resistant than women to some
pressures of mass society. For women have long
known how to live secret lives, how to give lip service
and even physical obedience to principles and people
for whom they had no real respect and still retain
something of their own point of view.[3] This hidden
resistance does not seem congenial to men, or rather
to the role that men, in our culture, are traditionally
supposed to play. Yet, unless he chooses to "knock

his head against a stone wall," many a man is likely
to learn to accept modification of the traditional role.
This may entail psychological difficulty. It may even
cause damage. Yet the lesson, once mastered, may
help some people to protect themselves against abdication of individuality and submergence in the
other-directed organizational society which talks about
teamwork and lives by cutthroat competition. Another
environment might be more wholesome, but struggling
to create it might require men to develop commitment
to programs for change—and they have been taught
to distrust such programs. To want the cake of comfort, to be aware of the cost of getting that cake, to be
reluctant to act to lessen the cost—this is the situation
which contemporary men must face and resolve in
order to cope with threats to their masculinity.

Versions of Sublimation

Contemporary society demands more of the male,
then, and gives him decreasingly effective psychological support to meet those demands. Displays of courage and physical strength have won men distinction
in war ever since men have engaged in organized
fighting. But modern war, even counterguerrilla actions, give relatively small scope for individual hero-
ism. Displays of shrewdness and judgment have won
men success in business and politics. But modern business offers a rather shrinking field to the individual who
wants to become a great entrepreneur rather than an
eminent corporation bureaucrat, and modern politics
has small place for the "loner." The boy is required to
be both aggressive and effective but his aggressiveness
must often be indirect in order to be effective, although he continues to be *told* that forthright self-
assertion is the only properly masculine attitude. This
anomalous situation increases inner conflicts; boys

find it harder to learn how to become adults and adult males find it more difficult to behave in masculine fashion.

A significant response to this confused condition is the development of distorted expressions of sexuality. The psychotherapist might classify these distortions as passivity, impotence—sexual and psychological—and homosexuality (both as something feared by individuals and as a phenomenon which is on the increase).[4] Before dealing with true distortions of sexuality, we may at least refer to some exaggerations of sublimation, such as the intense devotion to sports which seems to pass the bounds of mere pleasurable interest and become a kind of obligation. Every outdoor sport from boating to skiing apparently has followers enough to support at least one journal. Fishing has its devotees, ranging from lower-class males who use the attempt to catch a few porgies as an excuse for a comfortable day's beer-drinking away from wives and families, to the men with sufficient money to seek out water clean enough for fish to live in and with sufficient energy to hang on to the creatures they have hooked. Other kinds of sexual sublimation can be seen in the continued popularity of such spectator sports as football, hockey, boxing, and even that peculiar performance called professional wrestling.

Then there is verbal sublimation, as indicated by the rising circulation of magazines appealing to *male* readers in a rather different way from the old pulps which printed "action" stories. Today's pulps, *Man to Man, Real Man, Wildcat, The Man's Book,* and the like, are written in even simpler language than their predecessors and offer material far more overtly sexual. The older magazines concentrated on danger, hairbreadth escapes, feats of strength or endurance; their contemporary counterparts present luridly described heterosexual encounters coupled with old-fashioned violence, often becoming blatant sadism.

One might consider the men's magazines of the 1920's and 1930's to be ready-made fantasies addressed to semiliterate young males restive under the restrictions of dull, confining city jobs and eager to see themselves, in imagination, at least, as men of action —brave detectives, valiant Indian fighters, sturdy lumberjacks, stouthearted contractors and salesmen who defeated rivals and made fortunes for themselves. Today's Walter Mittys, however, identify themselves with heroes of higher social position. Their fantasies give sex "equal time" with action; less often do they describe their characters in the act of getting ahead in the world or making money. Yet the advertisements in today's male magazines show a remarkable resemblance to those printed earlier: "art" photos, muscle builders, virility builders, remedies for VD, courses that will lead to a better job; essentially the same promises addressed to the same pathetically frustrated reader.

Another sublimation of distorted sexuality may be seen in the current male preoccupation with automobiles. Again, this is not new. Rather, it is a further development of the interest in machines and of the mechanical ingenuity which has characterized Americans since Colonial gunsmiths invented (or at least creatively modified) the gun with a rifled rather than a smooth-bore barrel. Certainly, ever since the automobile came into common use in the United States, men, especially young men, have tinkered with their cars. A product of the assembly line, this triumph of standardized mass production has been, if not transformed by individual handling, at least often treated in a particularly personal manner. On the one hand (with the efflorescence of the "annual model" racket), we have seen men buying and discarding cars at regular intervals, with little real contact between ob-

ject and owner, and, on the other hand, we have
seen men who polish their cars with extraordinary
diligence, who tinker with the engine, who add all
sorts of "special" equipment to the indistinguishable
thing they have bought. Men have thus adorned and
improved their automobiles since the almost fabled
days of the Model T Ford.

Today, however, males seem to treat their cars in
a different fashion. Many still handle them as mere
commodities, useful for display of earning power and
status but not especially interesting in themselves.
Other males not only decorate and otherwise individ-
ualize their cars, but identify with them; these males
not only own their cars, they *are* their cars.[5] In and
through these machines they have power. Like that
"equalizer," the gun, the car, consciously or unconsciously, is a weapon, a means of assault on what may
be called the great feminine body of the world; one
need scarcely be a clinician to see a phallic symbol
in the automobile. Owning a car, like wearing the
standard uniform of the aspiring delinquent (blue
jeans, leather jacket, engineers' boots), demonstrates
to the world, and the owner, that indeed he does
have a penis in working order.

The more threatened the male may feel, the less
control over his own economic life, say, he is allowed
to exert, and the more he seems to be subordinated in
his home, the more he identifies with that image of
masculinity, the fast car, moving smoothly or noisily
down the highway, putting into his sometimes flabby
hands the power of a hundred horses so that the will
behind the wheel moves not only in strength, but if it
is heedless can even maim or kill.

Impotence

More overtly than in the sublimated guises just
sketched, distortions of sexuality are expressed in

impotence, passivity, and homosexuality, whether that is practiced or merely feared. Impotence has long been a male anxiety as potency has long been a source of male pride. Nowadays, impotence is of more than medical concern. The number of marriages made unhappy by male extramarital intercourse, is, one can venture, fewer than those wrecked by the male's inadequate sexual performance.

In my own practice, I find numerous instances of couples still in their forties who have simply abandoned sexual activity. Kinsey found that about 45 percent of all married men interviewed felt their performance to be inadequate.[6] Doctors Abraham and Hannah Stone suggest that about 10 percent of American men are impotent before they reach fifty and another 15 percent frustrate their wives by their failures.[7] Another observer suggests that 25 percent may be too low a figure for the proportion of impotent or inadequate males.[8]

Impotence is generally regarded as a psychosomatic phenomenon.[9] As Stekel wrote: "With normally developed genitalia and normal sex glands, there is no innate organically conditioned impotence, but only a psychic one; every form of local treatment is superfluous, at times dangerous, and usually injurious."[10]

Students of the problem tend to agree that most cases of sexual impotence are related to fear, envy, and guilt; the oedipal threat, the fear of castration, latent homosexuality, and hostility to the female, especially the wife, girl friend, or casual partner. The successful or the aggressive female arouses almost conscious hostility, especially in passive males, and they punish her with impotence. In our self-conscious age, when women pride themselves on their ability to rouse and satisfy their lovers, it is humiliating for a woman to have the male lose his erection. He may be humiliated, too, but he has the unconscious satisfaction of having rejected her. Such a rejection is the very sort of punishment the passive male would find gratifying: if he has cut off his nose to spite his face, he has, at least, saved that face, unconsciously, by the punishment he has inflicted. When, in psychotherapy, the passive male is distressed about episodes of impotence, he rarely expresses concern for the woman he has disappointed; his concern is for his own sense of masculinity.

The therapist still sees patients whose potency problems are related to the classical oedipal situation—identification of all women with the forbidden mother—and to modifications of that situation in which the desired, but tabooed mother, forbids her son to approach any other woman sexually. In this expression of the oedipal situation, the therapist sees another variation of the anxiety and hostility which so frequently helps cause the impotence of his male patients. Often, their relationship to their mothers has been of a kind that makes them fear women will attack the penis; they fear lest they be castrated. That fear is intensified by an unconscious awareness of their own hostility to women, and women in their turn become at least unconsciously castrating because their men are hostile, and in this way punish their men for sexual and social inadequacy. Such attitudes intensify the male's desire to reject and punish thus fostering the impotence which is the symbol of that hostility. The result is a truly vicious circle.

Again, this is not particularly novel: the "war between the sexes" is an age-old theme, but until the last few decades the discussion has been seasoned with a sense of superiority on the part of the males who engaged in it. Men might suspect that women laughed at them behind their backs, but is was possible for men to accept that suspicion because they were confident of their own essential eminence. Nowadays, that confidence seems to be diminishing among

American males. Thus we see not only physical impotence but a psychological impotence, expressed, although indirectly, in the sexual sphere. Much in the contemporary family situation, and certain factors in the economic world, lead to a high degree of competitiveness between men and women. If mate or lover achieves anything, socially or professionally, say, the other—in this case, the male—is roused to envy; and often he vents his hostility, which may be quite conscious, in sexual impotence.[11]

But psychological impotence may show itself in other ways. Dr. Karl Menninger remarks that men whose sexual behavior is mechanically adequate often experience only slight gratification; this low level of pleasure, he asserts, is "an unrecognized form of impotence."[12] If such absence of gratification becomes evident to the partner, as it may, then the relationship is clouded by further hostility, and again, an intimacy which should increase affection actually evokes antagonism and estrangement.

On another level, the male may be sexually adequate and even find satisfaction in sex, yet he may be so ineffectual in day-to-day living that his sexual potency seems a mere cloak for the psychological impotence he demonstrates. Here one verges on paradox, questioning whether sexual performance may not itself be a disguise for sexual impotence. In other words, a confidently potent male will also be able to confront his daily life efficiently; he will have command of his vocational skills; he will get along with other people; he will assert himself where assertion is appropriate but he will not be dedicated to belligerence as a way of proving to himself and others that he is a man. Such a person, consequently, will (the economy functioning in tolerably healthy fashion and the peace at least minimally secure) enjoy a measure of success in his day-to-day world. He may not earn a great deal of money, but he will probably earn enough to support a reasonably comfortable life. A man whose physical potency is a kind of psychosomatic cover-up, on the other hand, may well show this by his ineffectiveness in dealing with other problems. For him, sexual performance is a substitute for a larger social impotence. If one agrees that sexuality is a reflection of the character of one's being-in-the-world and one's commitment to the world, to use existentialist terms, then such complexities of psychological and psychosomatic behavior are not mere semantic play but rather a reflection of the male's tortuous relationships to reality.

Passivity

Psychological impotence may also be considered an aspect of male passivity, just as sexual impotence may be dealt with in terms of the latent homosexuality, which will be discussed later. We have talked of passivity earlier, but it is a sufficiently important phenomenon to warrant being discussed in another aspect. Psychoanalytically, the term "passivity" has wide ramifications. The concept is often used to give an instinctual explanation of neurosis and of "the neurotic character structures; failure of an individual to achieve active aims, or . . . his adhering to an older, defensive, gratifying position." [13] A substantial number of American males show this kind of passivity. Their character structure is colored by an often resentful and sometimes resisted dependency, upon mother or mother-substitute (who may be wife or lover), or upon the father if the father seems strong, although not sufficiently strong to have served as a model of masculinity with whom the son could have identified in attaining his own true manhood.

The link between passivity and dependence is important, for the American male is reared in a tradition where the father (in the dominant middle-class group) need not be authoritarian and where the son's relationship to his parents is not well defined. Because of this ambiguity, the young male is all but forced into a seductive relationship with his parents. Dependence, incidentally, entails more than mere clinging for support; rather, as sketched in an earlier chapter, dependency contains elements of both seductiveness and competition, with parents and children all vying for the attention and love of the others. All are rivals, in a way; all offer themselves to one another. In this fluid kind of relationship, where traditional roles have so changed that the family operates in new and unexpected ways, the oedipal conflicts are resolved, if resolved at all, only with the greatest difficulty.

To put it differently, the male too often is incapable of detaching himself from father or mother. This constitutes a dependence and, at the same time, is a form of passivity. The male seeks to reestablish such a relationship in involvements with other men and women in his life; he seeks associations where there is a great deal of "feeding" on the part of both parties, and a kind of mutual hampering of male activity. As mentioned earlier, this kind of passivity may be expressed in impotence, where the male, by being sexually inadequate, shows his hostility and even, perhaps, a kind of unconscious resentment at having to be active.

Passivity is strikingly expressed in other kinds of interpersonal relationships—the father whose link to his children is principally a monetary one—and on the job. Frequently, the passive male cannot assert himself at home. At work, he hesitates to accept the responsibility of making decisions on his own; he feels more comfortable in a group, where no one person can be held to account, or in a situation where he can attribute error to someone else. In "gamesmanship," which once was a joke but which has become a fine art in the struggle for economic and social success, victory and reward may well go not to the most competent in performance, but rather to the most skillful at putting blame on others while drawing credit to oneself.

The traditional image of the American male, strong, hardheaded, decisive, does not apply to the majority of contemporary men. The description might better be applied to American culture generally, since that often appears rather rigid, compulsive, and aggressive. Because the culture has this character, it operates to heighten male passivity, if only because the culture as a whole, not a man's own desire, determines his goals. This aspect of passivity cannot be regarded merely as individual neurotic behavior; it is much more a cultural phenomenon. In a highly organized society whose economy is dominated by the great, bureaucratically structured corporations and whose education so often resembles a kind of industrial processing, it is difficult for the male to take genuine initiative in the conduct of his life.[14]

At this point in discussing passivity, one should distinguish activity from initiative. Activity is an American syndrome; the American male has long been noteworthy for his absorption in strenuous work and equally strenuous bouts of diversion. In terms of real decisions, however, he is often essentially passive and this in areas ranging from politics and business to the conduct of his family life. In contemporary business, where the American male is most likely to work, initiative often does not mean proposing and carrying through some plan or idea leading to real innovation. Some room may be allowed for new ideas and concepts, but their novelty must not be obtrusive, the new proposal should not entail any fundamental departure from prevalent ways of thinking and behaving in the firm. There is to be no shaking of the foundations.

In politics and the conduct of social life, conformity and passivity are not unrelated. Acceptance of the status quo and resentment when its premises are questioned seem to underlie the whole consensual philosophy formulated by contemporary American historians and political scientists. To raise questions about fundamental issues—the nature and morality of contemporary patterns of property ownership, for example—is considered both foolish and discourteous; it denies the essential rightness of things as they are. To have a coherently enunciated set of general principles and a program for carrying them into action constitutes ideology and, to many contemporary academicians, ideology is a mental cancer. Even to imply that fundamental conflicts exist in American society (or have existed in the past) seems to create unreasonable disquiet in those who proclaim "the consensus." Almost one wonders whether there may not be a "reverse culture lag," whether the fear of "disloyal elements" which the American man-in-the-street has shown at intervals since 1919 may now have filtered upward.[15] It seems noteworthy that in the revival of what has been called *conservatism* since the 1950's, quite well-educated younger men are, according to Professor Hofstadter's study of *The Paranoid Style in American Politics*[16] showing some of the same psycho-political anxieties which troubled the fundamentalists of the 1920's.

Discussion in earlier chapters has shown the American male playing a passive role in his relationships with women and with his family. Frequently, when the male cannot maintain his preferred attitude of non-involvement, he tends either to retreat from women or to let them make the decisions. Betty Friedan quotes a correspondent of the New York *Village Voice* who wrote that the current question was not whether

blacks were good enough to marry whites, or contrariwise, but whether "women are good enough to
marry men, since women are on the way out." Certainly, one can see evidence of social passivity in the aban-
donment of public for private themes, a tendency
American novelists and playwrights share with their
fellow writers the world over. Our writers, however,
often couple this with a picture of the male who is the
passive object of female manipulation.¹⁷ That supposedly commendable woman who is set up against the
predatory and possessive female is usually some instance either of arrested sexual development or of
precocious and mindless promiscuity. Contrasted with
Hedda Gabler, we have not Candida or even Cordelia
but a willing Juliet who asks nothing of her lover,
not even affection.

The passive male, in my opinion, is more hostile to
women than is the active and aggressive male. This
may be a result of his inability to accommodate himself and his expectations to the real contemporary
woman. The passive male's mother was frequently the
powerful figure in his family and her behavior encouraged his dependence. When the boy, growing
into a passive adult, moves into the larger social world,
he learns that other women are not entirely like his
mother; they may want to dominate, yet they also
want challenge. Contemporary women are looking for
lovers and husbands, yet they are often asked to be
mothers. If they refuse the role, women often find
themselves estranged from the men with whom they
become involved. They do not wish to play the man's
role (even the role of a passive man), yet they cannot return to the old position of serving the male ego
(a position where they might, perhaps, be more tol-
erable to the passive male). For although today's
middle-class woman may have retreated to a suburban
kitchen and more children than her mother bore (a

retreat Professor Eli Ginzberg asserts is made by choice, when it is made), she may have spent time earning a living and she knows that she may have to return to work in order to assist in the education of her family and in supporting her children when they enter marriage and parenthood. Neither for her nor her husband can marriage be the old-fashioned "settling down."

A further reason for the anger which the passive male feels toward women is the compulsory and compulsive character of heterosexuality in contemporary culture. Everywhere—in the exhibitionist appeals of the advertisers, in mass-media entertainment, even in serious literature—women, the passive male feels, are thrust upon him. He is not only invited but, in effect, commanded to take possession. If he does not want to, he feels not in danger of loss but actually deprived; castration is no longer a threat, it is all but a *fait accompli.*[18] For reassurance, he is apt to lay excessive stress on the trappings of a masculinity he does not truly believe he has.

Thus, passivity becomes a distortion of sexuality and one generating a high degree of conflict. The passive male wants to rest upon the mother's bosom and be fed. Yet, at the same time, he wants to be a man, to be powerful. But he cannot have power and passivity together unless, like a woman, he turns passivity itself into a weapon by which he can acquire power. If he accepts and employs woman's weapons, can the passive male feel psychologically masculine?

Homosexuality

Homosexuality is the final distortion of sexuality[19] to be considered. Male passivity is, at least in part, a reflection of a culture which makes a new set of demands upon all human beings, demands which apparently require more adaptation by the man than by the woman. Male impotence, sexual or psychological, can usually be dealt with in psychotherapy. When that impotence is the outcome of unconscious latent homosexuality, however, the therapist's task becomes far more difficult.

First, what is "latent" homosexuality? Salzman, noting that latency has two aspects, dormancy and potentiality, notes that, in respect to homosexuality, latency means only dormancy: "The individual has hidden inside himself, a fully grown and developed capacity to be homosexual that covertly influences his behavior and attitudes." Dormant homosexuality is presumed to be part of everyone's personality structure, although it may be more apparent in some people than in others. The spread of Freudian influence among educated people in the United States, Salzman continues, has tended to make many males who experience sexual inadequacy translate normal concern over episodes of impotence into "obsessive rumination" and then to transform such rumination into fear of "latent homosexuality." This fear is said to be less prevalent among the lower-income groups and in cultures which have not been much affected by Freudian thought. Awareness of dormant homosexuality, Salzman contends, has as a concomitant the possibility of awakening the tendency.[20]

One need not attribute awareness of a dormant trend to the influence of psychotherapy. There is much in many men's behavior that might indicate to them they are strongly attracted to other males. They are enthusiastic alumni, given to noisy reunions. They play golf or go off on hunting and fishing expeditions that generally exclude women. They take to hobbies like target shooting that are masculine in character and principally attract men to them. This again may be an escape from women.[21] Finally, they even enjoy army life. (How many professional soldiers have either volunteered for military training or stayed in the armed forces after the term for which they were drafted because barracks life in continuous proximity to other men gratified their dormant homosexuality?)

Doubt about potency, incidentally, does not invariably lead psychologically sophisticated males to suspect that they are homosexual. Nor is it only upper-income males who feel threatened by dormant homosexuality. Cannot one explain the ferocious antagonism to homosexuals which is seen among some lower-class men as a typical reaction protecting the ego against a feared eruption of forces from within? Indeed, one might argue that the high tolerance for outbursts of masculine anger on this social level—and the taste for physical violence which prevails there—constitute a thinly disguised expression of homosexuality.

Realistically, it is among lower-class groups that masculinity is most important for the man. Perilously situated, socially and economically, as the lower-class male is apt to be, he may easily come to believe that he has but one possession belonging to him and him alone— not even the installment company to which he is in debt can repossess his penis. From the psychoanalytic point of view, few males grow up under circumstances that leave them relatively free of castration anxiety. Life in the lower-class family, where physical punishment is a frequent form of discipline (and one often administered by the father) and where prudishness is not uncommon, does not tend to ease the male child's castration fears. Again the economic position of the lower-class male, adolescent or adult, is in a constantly precarious state: even unionized blue-collar workers stand in danger of having the market for their skills eliminated either by the industrial engineers or by automation. These are the people whose income, and social position dependent on it, are most liable to attrition. In the United States, lower-class males are also the people whose traditional family structures have been most violently affected by the experience of moving from a static agricultural society into one shaped by rapid technological change.

Hence, the American lower-class male is unlikely to be more secure in his sense of masculinity than is the male of the middle class. He may be less able (and perhaps less willing) to put his fear of his homosexual propensities into words, but he is not therefore unaware of them. Clinical experience leads me to conclude that Italian males, for example, are particularly troubled by fear of homosexuality. Among Negroes, too, males feel threatened in their masculinity. Here, of course, special social factors—for example, the female-governed household with the father often actually, rather than merely psychologically, absent—come into play. Is it without significance that Negro slang calls individuals who are symbols of social authority—the boss at work, the policeman on the street—"the Man"? [22]

Dormant homosexuality is to be found among all segments of society then, and the increasing incidence of overt homosexuality may be general in its impact. In the situation described throughout this book, the male feels himself threatened by the demands of society, by the internal tensions generated during the course of his development and in his current experience, and by the need to cope with independent, self-assured women. The history of both male and female homosexuals, incidentally, frequently reveals families with assertive, domineering mothers who develop strong ties of affection with their sons, and with fathers who are weak in dealing with their wives and either hostile or indifferent to their sons. [23] The male unconsciously fears castration and consciously questions his own self-confidence, assertiveness, and capacity to make decisions. Under such circumstances, the male may feel anxiety in seeking the female, for he fears she will try to control him in the sexual encounter and as a consequence of that encounter. In contrast, another male seems safe. Although the homosexual experience *may* be fleeting, neurotic, even compulsive, it does not tie down either partner. Even when involvement is less compulsive and less neurotic, an attachment to another male constitutes less of a commitment than would commitment to a female, if only because there can be no children.

Today's world seems unstable; hence the impermanence of so many homosexual involvements seems merely to carry one step further the transitory nature of heterosexual attachments, including marriages. The homosexual partnership thus seems to fit the needs of many contemporary males. American society has become less punitive in its attitudes towards such partnerships so that, for many, it is not too difficult to develop, within the homosexual world, a feeling of rootedness and belonging. For these males, the movement goes beyond what Abram Kardiner characterized as a "flight from masculinity." Now homosexual males seem less concerned about their masculinity than about the identity crisis which so many of them are experiencing. This experience they share with other people, male and female, heterosexual and homosexual.

Literate man naturally dreams of visual solutions to the problems of human differences.

 —MARSHALL MCLUHAN
 in *Understanding Media*

Personality is to be extricated from the loyalties which disintegrate it.

 —DONALD B. MEYER
 in "The Confidence Man"

Past and present often are painted beside each other in a distorted symbolic way.

 —JOOST A. M. MEERLOO in
 "The Time Sense in Psychiatry"

CHAPTER VIII

Confrontations and Prospects

Historians, in studying the phenomena of social change, have been much impressed with their impact on the groups and individuals which experienced them. Responses to such transitions have altered group and individual behavior in ways affecting society as a whole. In the United States, where we have the myth that climbing the social ladder is a duty as well as an opportunity, it has come as something of a shock, even to professional students of social myths, to realize that downward as well as upward mobility is a fact of life. When those who once enjoyed security and respect in the community have had this pleasant condition disturbed, their dissatisfaction may produce neurosis and occasion ferment. Societies, and especially rapidly changing societies like that of the United States, always have problems to be resolved. Both sensitivity to social evils and the readiness to act to remedy these are increased by the awareness that one's status is declining or that the position one has achieved is not actually bringing the expected reward, the deference and regard, which represent values in the community.

Two notable periods of American social ferment seem especially associated with status shifts: the exciting decades of the 1830's and 1840's, when restiveness was creatively expressed in many areas of social life, particularly in the protest against slavery, a protest which swelled from an outcry made by a small group to a force which could not be ignored, even by a society that, then as now, proclaimed its devotion to compromise and the achievement of consensus. A second period of protest and ferment occurred at the end of the nineteenth century and during the years before World War I. Here the focus of attention was economic, in considerable part, but economic change was demanded in the name and with the vocabulary of an outraged morality.[1]

Contemporary studies of leaders in the antislavery and Progressive movements show that an appreciable number of them were caught in what Professor Hofstadter in his *Age of Reform*[2] has described as a status revolution based on a transfer of the possession of money. This movement of money was accompanied by a change in the allocation of social prestige both in the leaders' local communities and in the nation as a whole. Established upper-level groups—ministers, lawyers, merchants, and their families, people who had had comfortable fortunes for years—were outstripped in earnings by bankers, exploiters of natural resources, railroad builders, manufacturers, and speculators in stocks. The established groups lost accordingly, because in a fluid society possessions are the most evident and accepted sign of personal worth. This was the more true in the United States, where making money was assumed to demonstrate that the enriched enjoyed the favor of God, or stood at the summit of the evolutionary process. Many among the displaced refused to accept the verdict and responded by active, organized protests against what they regarded as abuses in the society.

Clearly looking at American society as it has developed during the last eighty years and particularly since World War I, a revolution has occurred in the position of the sexes. In many respects the male has declined and the female has risen. The declining group has not found any easy way to express its protest in terms of attack on social abuses. Other factors

have operated to make any social protest less acceptable since the end of the 1930's—Americans have decided that, after all, they inhabit a social order which,
despite some weaknesses, certainly is built on the
best of all possible theories of government and produces the most admirable possible results. The United
States, after all, can show the world more of what
is worth having, from TV sets to college educations,
in the possession of more people than can aspire to
such treasures anywhere else. If it also shows whole
regions of economic depression and a very substantial
group of people committed to maintaining another
group in subjection, these are national blots which
could soon be erased by programs to bring the culturally deprived into the middle-class orbit. If the
nation is engaged in a singularly unattractive display
of military power against opponents who appear stubbornly unwilling to admit either their own weakness or
America's right to make them accept its view of their
good, this points up the great disparity between professed ideals and actual behavior.

With enthusiasm for social change still under something of a cloud (although the cloud has thinned a bit
since the 1950's), male disquiet in the face of loss of
status has tended to find expression in a variety of
neurotic responses. The psychotherapist who observes
the American male as he functions on the contemporary scene sees him as a person-in-crisis, an individual
who has lost a traditional position and not been able to
replace it with anything that begins to give him some
of the support and security which the old position
conferred.

The American male confronts a new version of the
female. An imaginative student of the past who, like
Robert Graves, does not trammel the imagination with
literal documentation, might say that "in the beginning" the female ruled. She was (to use Graves'
formula) Lady, Maiden, Hag, goddess of birth, of

love, of death. She governed inscrutably, as the earth is inscrutable, but her governance was directed toward fostering life and the most important manifestation of life, poetry. Then came the great revolution, the rising of the male against the domination of the female. That revolt succeeded: descent came to be reckoned through the father; it was *he* who killed and ruled, made the laws and created the poems, and possessed the intellectual tools.

Leaving the poet's vision of the dim past (a vision based on inference from the literary, artistic, and religious record read by a wilful spirit) for the facts of life in the nineteenth century, the male then confronted the female in a context which was clearly and firmly structured. He was on top. In society and in the family, he ran things. Men ruled the world: they alone voted and held office; they reserved professional and business employment for themselves; they almost had all the opportunities to acquire and use formal education. Women did write books, of course, but they were expected to produce novels or poems; philosophy and theology were for men.

In confronting the female, sexually and socially, the male took the lead: in parlor or brothel, he did the choosing. When marriage was in question he (or his representatives) took the initiative. He did the courting and the proposing. And where marriage was the only acceptable course for any but the exceptional middle-class woman (as it was in many instances even in the United States, where women had greater economic and social freedom than they did in western Europe), many women took the man's offer, not for his sake, but for the security and the status which marriage offered.

Within the home, the man was at least presumed to be the head of the family. He earned the family's income and controlled the spending of it. The woman, as wife and mother, had a recognized influence, but

much of that was by sufferance or achieved by guile.
It was for the male, as father and head of the family,
to make major decisions: where the family was to live
and on what standard of expense; how the children
should be educated; even, on occasion, whom they
should marry.

This was the situation as prescribed, of course; matters might proceed quite differently in fact. Many
husbands were "henpecked." Many women ruled their
families by strength disguised as submissive weakness.
Nevertheless, the male was presumed to exercise authority in the home as he did in the community.

Perhaps the most evident sign of male domination
during the nineteenth century was the character of the
sexual relationship. Only the man was considered entitled to satisfaction; women—especially middle-class
women—endured or, at best, accepted sex, they did
not expect to enjoy it. Females did not worry about
being frigid; males did not concern themselves with
gratifying their wives. Bruno Bettelheim declares that
such a matter-of-fact attitude about sex left the nineteenth-century female more free to conflict about
sexuality than her twentieth-century descendant.[3]
(This, of course, assumes that the attitude actually
was merely matter-of-fact and not colored by any
denigration of sexuality.) Certainly, by making fewer
demands on the male, the nineteenth-century attitude
left him better able to deem himself sexually adequate,
whatever his actual performance might be.

During the twentieth century, women began to assert their claim to gratification. What was sauce for
the gander should please the goose as well. Men responded to the demand, perhaps themselves relieved
to be free of the Victorian period's implicit charge that
they were really acting as oppressors in enjoying their
conjugal rights.

But the sexual emancipation that seemed to fore-
tell liberation and joy has proved, in many instances,

quite the opposite, and particularly for the male. In an
article which has some amusing undertones, Dr. Leslie
Farber portrays the pathetic yet ludicrous situation in
which many couples find themselves: they have been
told how they ought to feel and how their sexuality
ought to function. They have also been told that love
would make them more consistently efficient sexual
athletes. They do not perform according to prescription. Accordingly, they either do not really love each
other or they are neurotically inhibited.

The difficulty, Farber argues, arises because of the
notion that females are "entitled" to orgasm and males
are "obligated" to give it to them. As a result, what
should be spontaneously joyous has become a matter
of calculated technique—and sexuality is degraded by
being separated from the totality of existence and
transformed into a mechanized exercise of the will.[4]

The author, an existential psychoanalyst, is pro-
testing against the increasing divorce between sex
and life, and he illustrates his protest by an account
of the Masters laboratory study of the female in orgasm. Such studies, and the willingness of respectable
women to participate in them for a fee, Farber argues,
shows how completely enslaved we have become to
the notion that every aspect of life ought to be subject to the will, an object of manipulation and control.[5]

Sex will continue to be practiced, Farber admits,
but because it is becoming both depersonalized and
overpersonalized in the sense that the partners are too
eager to please each other on the performance level,
sex is losing its quality as an experience and surprise.

Farber's viewpoint may be a tenable one. But its
assertion that the existence of the female orgasm is at
least in part the product of a scientific study of sex,
and its protest against women's demand to experience
orgasm might be taken, by an acidulous female reader,
as testimony of male discomfort in the presence of

women who have decided that they have "rights" in bed as well as in the voting booth.

So times have changed. Middle-class women are no longer restricted to the rules of dutiful daughter, good wife, devoted mother, loving grandmother (to paraphrase contemporary death notices)—all of them more or less confined to home, church, and, in the upper-income, either frivolity or sober, religiously oriented amateur social work. Many aspects of the change were, of course, well under way before World War II. Women had won the right to vote and to hold public office; married women might own their own property and claim the guardianship of their own children. Women had established a claim to higher education. They were free to engage in the liberal professions, and those of the middle-class were expected to be self-supporting for at least a portion of their lives.

American men now face something more than a merely emancipated woman; they must deal with a female who is herself questioning the character of her relationship with the male. Many of today's women feel they should be capable of grappling with independent lives, lives which, naturally, have a place for the male but which do not necessarily focus on acquiring him as lover or husband or serving his needs as head of the family. These women are not rejecting the male, but some of them are coming to realize that they can do without the male in a number of situations. Since women now outnumber men, it is necessary for some women to plan lives which do not include marriage. Even women who count on being successful in the initial round of competition know that they may —before their children are grown—be obliged to live without the husband they lose by divorce.

The male is more and more aware of his own dissatisfaction with the narrowed range of experience which the contemporary pattern of early marriage imposes on him. The traditional family situation seems to cost more than it gives in love or stability. Pre-marital and extramarital sex have deprived marriage of its role as the sole provider of reliably present sexual partners. The home has long since ceased to produce anything essential to the economy (except new consumers, of course). Professional educators and counselors—and the peer group—have taken over most of the family's educational and socializing functions; the mother still rears her children, by and large, but she seeks, and gets, considerable assistance. The traditional family structure thus seems progressively less well adapted to the need of today's technological society.

What course that society takes will determine the character of the male's future vis-à-vis the female specifically and the social order generally. Technological change, with its impact upon the home and upon the patterns of economic life, has already markedly transformed the environment of the American male. He has lost his traditional position of secure dominance in family and society. What it is now is yet to be determined. When this state of uncertainty causes him to suffer, it is the consequence of the passing of old values without new values rising to replace them. Increasingly, it seems that the male will be compelled to exist as an independent individual without the support of a progressively unstable family group. New conceptions of masculinity and new ideas about the social role of the male will evolve. It seems likely that the future will bring images of masculinity no less shattering than those which have occurred during the past three decades. With even further weakening of family bonds, a person will need to become more secure within himself. Education will have to be altered in such a way as to foster an autonomy which is the only possible safeguard against a growing alienation so many young males seem to be not merely experiencing but actually cultivating.[6] Unless contemporary

society can help them prepare for a psychologically
new position and a new social role, their plight will be
rapidly intensified.

Political and educational leadership, however, seems
preoccupied with drawing more and more young people, especially from among the poor, into the orbit of
middle-class values. Psychotherapists can testify to
the number of middle-class youngsters who find those
values irrelevant. For example, in a world where
spending is more useful to the economy than saving,
and where attention to business has led to such disregard of the natural and social environment that it
becomes increasingly hard to find breathable air,
drinkable water, earth uncontaminated by chemical
residues, and fire which does not poison the wind
with its by-products, they are not attracted by ideals
of thrift and prudence. Thus, in many instances, there
is a great divorce between the generations, with many
potentially creative young males so disaffected that
they are not merely in rebellion, but in flight, pre-
ferring the world of hallucination produced by drugs
to the confrontation of reality with all of its problems.

For the future, the male faces this final question:
Can he develop a new concept of his social role and
adequate psychological support to confirm him in his
conviction of his identity as a male? Can he do this
in time to create a new confidence in his masculinity?
One can scarcely consider the negative: that would
imply the flagging of the human capacity to adapt.
Yet what evidence is there that the capacity to adapt
actually does exist in the contemporary American male,
or in the larger social and existential context in which
he has his being?

Jeder Mensch ist eine kleine Gesellschaft.
[Every man is a society by himself.]

NOVALIS

CHAPTER IX

The Future of
American Man:
What Can Be done?

There are obviously no ready-made solutions for the plight of the American man. However we shall try to develop some ideas in this chapter, which might serve as an aid to a possible redefinition and readjustment of the position of the American man.

In thinking about a new definition and place for the American man it certainly would not be any good to return to the past. Gone are the days when father knew best and even at work he no longer commands the power he had in the past.

What opportunities are still left for him in the post-industrial, technological society? What can possibly be his place in an increasingly depersonalized society? What role is there left for him in a family where his word is no longer taken for granted?

Does he have to look for a new masculinity—as some observers have suggested—or should he detach himself from former concepts of masculinity and look altogether for new forms which will constitute a new character?

Depersonalization versus "Becoming a Person"

Throughout this book we have stressed the depersonalizing elements in our culture and their effects upon the role of the contemporary American man. Depersonalization implies that the individual in a given society, i.e., the American society, does not express

and experience those qualities which make one feel a
person. Offhand there is the idea of dignity. The depersonalization of the American man has robbed him
of his dignity as a man. Dignity by no means implies
"dignified" or "being established." It has a particular
meaning of being valued, of esteem and regard. In
the process of dealing with the technological society
the American man has to find once again that feeling
of dignity and esteem which once was his. He should
be proud of his being a man, of his role in whatever
period of time he finds himself. He should insist upon
acknowledgment by his peers and wife and children.
No longer should he be satisfied to accept the common
notions about his masculinity and his choice of action.
Such a course, naturally, requires *responsibility*, which
should be his key word for the decades to come. No
longer should he allow himself to be stripped of his
responsibilities, but rather should insist upon them.
Without becoming a bully he can and should exercise
his worth as being a man and—father.

The Possibility of Choice

The contemporary American male all too often for-
gets that he does not have to comply with the structure
of his society *per se*. Within the vast complex network
of modern society there are still possibilities of *choice*.
For a man who wants to be autonomous, the realiza-
tion of *choice* is sometimes shattering,[1] since for decades he has been seduced by the notion that "we cannot do anything about it" or "society is stronger" and,
again, "you'll have to conform." No American by himself will bring about a revolution in the structure of
our society, but nevertheless he can and should look
for opportunities, at home, at work and in his social
setting, where he can feel "I have done that" and "I
am *responsible*." The emasculation of the American
man, I repeat, does not only take place within the

realm of sexual performance, but even more so within his larger environment. The stress upon choice will also bring about his renewed confrontation with his family. No longer should he divorce himself from it but instead try to become a vital member of that family, to insist upon being heard and acknowledged. Two key words stand out in any meaningful family relationship: *cooperation* and *integration*. A man should not consider himself removed from the family structure; he must insist upon being taken into it and he must assume his responsibilities within it.

The Revival of Spontaneity

In the renewed effort to rediscover the family the male and father should also take heed of a new sense of *spontaneity* and *adventure*. No longer should he and his family (or for that matter the single male and his friends) feel that they have to conform to the usual patterns of behavior. Spontaneity means adventure and discovery and the American man should look around and make a serious effort to *relax* and, so to say, sit down or for that matter take a walk with his children! A new exciting area of play and leisure can be innovated within the cities, suburbs and even in the country.[2]

In the interaction with family and others the elements of *care* and *relaxation* should be stressed. Care implies *regard* for one's personality and the dignity of that personality. Relaxation stands for an *ease* which should accompany the actions of the person; he should feel free and unconstrained in his approaches and attitudes toward family, associates and friends.

Counterattack Upon the Disruptive Forces

The disruptive forces in society, as expressed in anomie, violence and an increasing disregard for the human being, are of course ready to fight the positive attitudes of the person, who is determined not to be taken in by the disintegration of society. The individual, and this has always been one of my strong convictions, *is able* to decide for himself, although sometimes in a limited context, the course he wants to take. In this course he has to avail himself, and this certainly applies to American male, of such characteristics as relaxation and ease. In other words, the rigidity which has been prescribed by contemporary society has to be dealt with. He should refuse to be intimidated with rigid approaches at home, work and in the society at large. Rigidity in contemporary society has become a defense against the spontaneous forces of man, forces which are still alive and need only to be revived and reinforced.

A quotation from Novalis comes to mind in discussing the rigidity of our contemporary society and man. "Every man is a society by himself." This means that he is *in charge* and that in the interaction with others he can afford to relax and *enjoy* marriage, sex, work and other human relationships. The more he heeds prescription, the less he will be in control. While control does not have to mean rigidity, there is the element of that danger. But the man who has come to terms with himself and recognizes himself for what he is, will also be able to exercise control in a relaxing fashion. This all calls for a reduction in the anxiety-provoking forces in our society. Too often we are inclined to panic about our human relationships, our work and other concerns. We seem to feel that we cannot sit down, which in effect we should, and contemplate the pressures. Pressures are all too often *reflections* of our inner insecurity, which in turn we tend to support.

A new masculinity for the male does not require sexual potency *per se* or an exhibition of his masculine qualities, but it requires in the decades to come a sense of *decision, choice, ease, calm* and comfort with himself. We must not fool ourselves that the problems of contemporary American man can be solved by prescription; they only can be solved ultimately in the renewal of man and the rediscovery of his sense of dignity.

CHAPTER I

1. Here, and probably throughout the book, we shall be talking of the middle-class woman. Such concentration is not a sociological distortion because, in the United States, everyone either thinks he belongs to the middle class or aspires to move into that class. Except for the nonwhite minorities whom the society as a whole is beginning to seek to assimilate, Americans accept middle-class mores as their own. The afflictions of middle-class people, therefore, tend to filter down through the social structure, and to do so more quickly than would be true in most European countries.

2. See, for example, Betty Friedan, *The Feminine Mystique* (New York: Dell, 1964); Phyllis and Eberhard Kronhausen, *The Sexually Responsive Woman* (New York: Ballantine, 1965); Oriana Fallaci, *The Useless Sex* (New York, Horizon, n.d.); Lena Levin and David Loeth, *The Emotional Sex* (New York: Morrow, 1964); Elizabeth Mann Borgese, *Ascent of Woman* (New York: Braziller, 1962); Farber and Wilson (eds.), *The Potential of Woman* (New York: McGraw-Hill, 1963); H. R. Hays, *The Dangerous Sex* (New York: Putnam, 1964); "Woman in America" (*Daedalus*, Spring, 1964).

3. My friend Bill Lindh, in an unpublished paper, "The Forty Syndrome," writes about the forty-year-old man in the following words: "He is sold laxatives that are designed for the intestinal tract that even knows its age (over 35); he is sold underarm deodorants that the athletes use, hair lotion, perfume (called cologne); from the top of his head to his toenails he is all market. Around him swirl the explosive theories of the 'Female Mystique'—he has failed to be the male his wife needs, his family suffers from his shortcomings and his supervisor finds him uncreative."

4. Robert P. Odenwald, *The Disappearing Sexes* (New York: Random House, 1965), p. 76.

5. Marshall McLuhan, *Understanding Media* (New York:

McGraw-Hill, 1965), p. 349.

6. Alexis de Tocqueville, *Democracy in America* (New York: Vintage, 1959), Vol. II, pp. 144–45.

7. Erik Erikson, "Inner and Outer Space: Reflections on Womanhood" (*Daedalus*, Spring, 1964), p. 582.

8. Edward Ziegler, "Payment by Status" (*Nation*, Vol. 191, November 12, 1960).

9. David Riesman, *The Lonely Crowd* (New Haven: Yale University Press, 1961), pp. 113–14.

10. Leslie Farber, *The Ways of the Will* (New York: Basic Books, 1966); see Chapter III, "I'm Sorry, Dear," p. 51.

CHAPTER II

1. The asexual Victorian lady may be more literary convention than fact, to be sure, but she was a useful social artifact, whatever psychological damage she may have wrought in the long run.

2. Allen Wheelis, *The Quest for Identity* (New York: Norton, 1958), p. 20.

3. André Gide, *If It Die* (New York: Vintage, 1963), pp. 10–11.

4. Max Brod, *Franz Kafka: A Biography* (New York: Schocken Books, 1963), pp. 19–20.

5. Irving and Jean Stone, eds., *Dear Theo* (New York: Grove Press, 1960), pp. 25–26.

6. And indeed, many a confirmed bachelor of an earlier day may have been a homosexual relatively unaware of his problem and not often expressing his needs in overt behavior.

7. In current teenage fashion, a great deal of emphasis is placed on the masculine and rugged elements such as the reintroduction and rediscovery of jeans and broad leather belts.

8. Young men still find it possible to have nineteenth-century virtues, of course. Consider this description of a famous Princeton basketball player: Bill is "very much in the Victorian tradition—his rationality, *morality*, his taking responsibility, his commitment to religious goals. He's always got a goal he's after. He's always out to accomplish something." (*Newsweek*, March 15, 1965; italics mine.) Another description of the old-fashioned ideal American male is offered in *Holiday's* interview "Diemer True, Young Conservative" (March, 1965, p. 48). But the type is becoming scarce; the alienated young man is more common on the American college campus than the "all-American boy."

9. For those readers who have read Truman Capote's *In Cold Blood* the figure of Mr. Clutter seems to appear as the ideal American man and father. However, Diana Trilling in her

brilliant review of the book in *Partisan Review* (Spring, 1966, pp. 258–59) writes the following interesting observations about Mr. Clutter, which in my opinion apply to quite a few American men: "Indeed, for me, by far the most interesting aspect of Mr. Capote's book as an American story lies not in the gratuitous violence of the crime it describes—this is not an American invention, though it is as ready at hand for us as if it were—nor in the dreary circumstances of the lives of Smith and Hickock—of this we already have some knowledge—but in the curious ambiguous personality of Mr. Clutter. If Mr. Capote is at all a novelist in this book, it is, paradoxically enough, as an accident of his entirely literal reporting of this highly 'masculine' character undone by his passivity and by—if you will—his lack of actual identity. One is reluctant (it seems like chic) to draw so exemplary a citizen, a successful teetotaling Republican devout progressive farmer, into the circle of self-alienated Americans. Yet manifestly this was a man without connection with his inner self, living by forced intention, by conscious design, programmatically, rather than by any happy disposition or natural impulse. His response to anger could not have been more contemporary in its 'enlightened' propitiatoriness and in its lack of instinctual manliness. Otherwise, would it not have allowed for something other than the guilt-ridden reaction—if these people less fortunate than himself wanted his money, he must give it to them—which was his only reaction to an invasion of his home? Mr. Clutter was a towering figure in his community. One of the last things said to him on the day of his death was said by a neighbor: 'Can't imagine you afraid. No matter what happened, you'd talk your way out of it.' This sounds like a compliment to courage. But then one thinks of what is actually implied in the idea that we now can define fearlessness as the ability to 'talk your way out of' danger: is there nothing beyond the reach of reasonable persuasion? Certainly Mr. Clutter was a talker—not a conversationalist—and this is an American and contemporary thing to be. But according to most folk wisdom, it is also not a very masculine thing to be; it is not supposed to go along with power, force or any other older principle of manliness. In men who had come to his home 'to splatter hair on the walls,' Mr. Clutter confronted a spirit which he was unprepared to meet and before which he was fatally disarmed."

CHAPTER III

1. *Newsweek*, March 21, 1966, pp. 62–63. The effort made to assure (and so reassure) readers that "The Teen-Agers" was

based on valid material is in itself interesting. Adults evidently want to be told that all is well with the high-school set, that, on the whole, they like their parents, they are not interested in politics, they enjoy shopping, and they believe in God.

2. *Ibid.*, p. 72.

3. Reuel Denney, "American Youth Today: A Bigger Cast, A Wider Screen," (*Daedalus,* Winter, 1962), p. 162.

4. Paul Goodman, *Growing Up Absurd* (New York: Random House, 1961), pp. 99–100.

5. Kenneth Keniston, "Social Change in Youth in America" (*Daedalus,* Winter, 1962), p. 163.

6. Phyllis Grosskurth, *The Woeful Victorian: A Biography of John Addington Symonds* (New York: Holt, Rinehart and Winston, 1965), pp. 1, 9–15, 60–61, 143, 150, 246. The irony of the elder Symonds' refusal to allow his son to be effeminized by learning music is sharpened when one reads how the boy grew up to be tormented all his life long by the conflict between his father's, and his society's, ideal of masculinity and his own homosexual needs.

7. For the interested reader it might be worthwhile to note that in the country of my origin (Holland) a flood of literature concerned with the father-son relationship has erupted in the last decade. Some examples are the books by Jan Wolkers, e.g., *Terug Naar Oegstgeest* and *Kort Amerikaans,* and Gerard Kornelis van het Reve, i.e., *De Avonden.*

8. Carl and Sylvia Grossman, *The Wild Analyst* (New York: George Braziller, 1965), pp. 1, 19, 72, 105. See also Martin Grotjahn's excellent essay on Groddeck in *Psychoanalytic Pioneers,* edited by Franz Alexander *et al.* (New York: Basic Books, 1966); see page 308, "The Untamed Analyst."

9. Max Brod, *Franz Kafka: A Biography* (New York: Schocken Books, 1965).

10. This had not always been true; Congreve, in the seventeenth century, shows father and son all but rivals for the same woman. And French comedy of that period does not scruple to show fathers as miserly old spoilsports and sons dedicated to deceiving and exploiting them.

11. Howard Wolf, "British Fathers and Sons, 1773–1913: From Filial Submissiveness to Creativity" (*Psychoanalytic Review,* Summer, 1965).

12. Samuel Butler, *The Way of All Flesh* (New York: Modern Library, 1950), p. 31.

13. The attitude of the American working-class father—who remains closer to his ethnic background—toward sons who are moving away from that background as they climb the social ladder has not been much investigated: curiously, in a country

characterized by social mobility, comparatively few studies
have been made of that mobility as it affects relationships between fathers and sons in families with immigrant grandparents.

14. The child-rearing expert tells mothers and fathers how
to "parent" (to coin still another barbarism), thus serving as
grandparent-surrogate. The nursery-school teacher may be a
mother-surrogate; the Scoutmaster may serve as surrogate father. And if the experts to whom parents turn—the teachers,
group leaders, minister-counselors, and the like—do not succeed, then the psychotherapist takes over.

15. *Cf.* Irving Kristol, "The 20th Century Began in 1945"
(*New York Times Magazine*, May 2, 1965).

16. See my lecture, "Identity and Social Change: Implications
for Parents" (New York: The Childhood Study Association of
America, in press).

17. Dick Hendrikse, *De Dag Waaop Mijn Vader Huilde*
(Haarlem: *De Spaarnestad*, 1965), pp. 5–6 (my translation).

18. It is again interesting to note here that Victorian and pre-
Victorian fathers in their zeal to accomplish success for their
sons did *not* become strangers. On the contrary, the son became
almost an extension of papa. Brigid Brophy, in her study
Mozart: The Dramatist, describes in Chapter XXI the nature
of Mozart's relationship with his father, Leopold Mozart: "The
influence of Leopold Mozart, forever driving Mozart to rebel
and forever pulling him back on the strings of filial piety,
could not be removed by physical distance (which was bridged
by letters) or even finally by Leopold's death. The father was
indeed eternal—in the son. And equally Mozart was eternally a
son: a personality, an Ego, whose existence was psychically possible only in and through the filial relationship . . . with proud
obedience and as a proof that he was doing as Leopold wanted
him to do: 'I am most attentive to my duty. I am quite a second
Papa.'" (*Mozart: The Dramatist*, New York: Harcourt, Brace
and World, 1964, pp. 258–59.)

19. If we are to take the fashions of the mid-1960's as an
indication, the American adult (especially the adult woman)
wants to look like an adolescent and is quite willing to behave
like one. In years, she often actually is all but an adolescent,
for the median age at marriage has dropped into the very
early twenties or even the late teens—and this when the school-
leaving age has risen, at least for white persons.

20. We should remember, nonetheless, that in many suburban
settings, peers will not be of strikingly different socioeconomic
backgrounds. American life is apparently becoming more stratified, however homogenized it may look to the outsider.

21. Kenneth Keniston, *op. cit.*

22. Erik Erikson, "Youth: Fidelity and Diversity," in *The Challenge of Youth* (New York: Doubleday Anchor Books, 1965), p. 11.

23. *New York Times Magazine,* June 13, 1965.

24. Yielding to this temptation might be taken as a factor in the cult of youth, which seems so incongruous in a society where old people are increasing in numbers and where the early forties (certainly mathematical middle age) seems to make a presidential candidate peculiarly youthful.

25. Kenneth Keniston, "Inburn: An American Ishmael," in Robert W. White, ed., *The Study of Lives* (New York: Atherton Press, 1963), pp. 40–70.

26. See also Kenneth Keniston, *The Uncommitted: Alienated Youth in American Society* (New York: Harcourt, Brace and World, 1965).

27. *Holiday,* March, 1966, pp. 46–47.

28. J. H. van den Berg, *The Changing Nature of Man* (New York: W. W. Norton and Co., 1961), p. 169.

29. I am less concerned, as far as young males are concerned, about sexual promiscuity. After all, at least there is the contact with another person. What concerns me more is the rather flippant defense of LSD as a cure for our troubles. The young man on "a trip" is in touch only with himself (if at that) and thus avoids confrontation with the world. If there is passivity among our young males, then LSD will only encourage it.

CHAPTER IV

1. In his *Brief an den Vater,* Kafka describes the old-fashioned and self-righteous father in the following words: "Your opinion was correct, every other one was distorted, overstrained, mad, abnormal. Your self-confidence was so great you could be wholly inconsistent and still be right."

2. See Norman Kelman, "Social and Psychoanalytic Reflections on the Father," in Hendrik M. Ruitenbeek, ed., *Psychoanalysis and Social Science* (New York: E. P. Dutton, 1962), p. 128.

3. Kenneth Keniston, *The Uncommitted: Alienated Youth in American Society* (New York: Harcourt, Brace and World, 1965), pp. 107–08, 160, 300, 488.

4. Karl Stern, *The Flight from Woman* (New York: Farrar, Straus, Giroux, 1965), pp. 1–3.

5. Thomas Szasz, "Legal and Moral Aspects of Homosexuality," in Judd Marmor, ed., *Sexual Inversion* (New York: Basic Books, 1965), p. 134.

6. Margaret Mead, *Male and Female* (New York: Morrow, 1949; New York: New American Library, 1955).

7. Generally, the provision is for the male who needs to behave as a female. The exterminated Mandan Indians of the Plains area of the United States institutionalized the provision in the *berdache,* a man who chose to live as a woman, wearing clothes like hers, doing her kind of work including quill embroidery, and often living in a spouse's relationship with another male. (We have no adequate account of a people who gave similar consideration to the woman who needed to live as a man.)

8. It may be a hazardous speculation, but perhaps American women are more aggressive mothers than their European contemporaries because they live in a more aggressive culture.

9. Helene Deutsch, "Ein Frauenschicksal: George Sand," in *Almanach für das Jahr 1929* (Vienna: Internationale Psychoanalytischer Verlag, 1929), p. 150.

10. Simone de Beauvoir, *The Second Sex* (New York: Knopf, 1953).

11. The figure of the bachelor uncle is in this context worth mentioning. In the twenties and thirties bachelor uncles were somewhat of an institution (at least in Europe) and often were considered the kind of benevolent surrogate father.

12. The date is quite arbitrary: in that year, the English firm of Boulton and Watt first operated a hammer in an iron works by steam power; and in that year, too, France and England signed a peace treaty which left the British dominant as a colonial power in two hemispheres and all but sole effective ruler of the sea. It was the beginning of the Industrial Revolution and Britain was entering on her troubled path to economic and political primacy; the nineteenth-century background was taking shape.

13. Karl Stern, *op. cit.,* pp. 273–74.

CHAPTER V

1. There has been, in my opinion, a rather distressing increase in the "mechanization" of food. Meals at one time were carefully prepared, and eaten, for that matter. In the affluent society it is no longer necessary for the family to share its meals and preparation has been reduced to a minimum.

2. The impact of the young upon contemporary fashion has become staggering in the last years. Carnaby Street in London has set the tone for a teenage fashion, which in turn has influenced to a great extent adult fashions.

3. Again, the segregation of the male is not novel. Men have long been accustomed to spend a good deal of their free time away from wife and children in some sheltered retreat—saloon, barbershop, poolroom, club, according to income—where a

man could be idle in the company of his peers, but that absence used to be considered something of a lapse from duty: the middle-class American father's leisure was supposed to be spent with his family in their home or, later, in their car. In much of the agitation for Prohibition, for example, a major reason given for abolition of the liquor trade was the need to protect the lower-class family from the saloon's attraction for the lower-class father who was beguiled not only by the alcohol but by the company it provided.

4. Sebastian de Grazia, *Of Time, Work, and Leisure* (New York: The Twentieth Century Fund, 1962), pp. 45–46.

5. William H. Whyte, Jr., *The Organization Man* (New York: Doubleday Anchor Books, 1956), p. 217. One might put Mr. Whyte's prose into something like modern verse, thus: "I loved my father and my mother, but / my father a little bit more. / I like things / pretty much the way they are. / I never worry much / about anything. / I don't / care for books or music much. / I love my wife and children but / I don't let them get in the way / of company work."

6. *Harvard Business Review*, January-February, 1954.

7. Perhaps blue-jeaned women and long-haired men are sufficiently certain of their sexual roles not to need external trappings for them. Perhaps masculine aggressiveness is unrelated to dullness of garb; the silks and laces and damasks of Elizabethan men adorned their undoubted maleness. Male animals, usually far gaudier than females, may display elegance of fur or plumage, ruffling of crests and manes, as signals of readiness to fight.

8. Donald Meyer, *The Positive Thinkers* (New York: Doubleday, 1965), p. 47.

9. Marshall McLuhan forecasts a workless and propertyless society in the decades to come as direct result of the electronic or computer age. I quote: "Such is also the harsh logic of industrial automation. All that we had previously achieved mechanically by great exertion and coordination can now be done electrically without effort. Hence the specter of joblessness and propertylessness in the electric age. Wealth and work become information factors, and totally new structures are needed to run a business or relate it to social needs and markets. With the electric technology, the new kinds of instant interdependence and interprocess that take over production also enter the market and social organizations. For this reason, markets and education designed to copy with the products of servile toil and mechanical production are no longer adequate. Our education has long ago acquired the fragmentary and piece-

meal character of mechanism. It is now under increasing pressure to acquire the depth and interrelation that are indispensable in the all-at-once world of electric organization." (*Understanding Media* [New York: McGraw-Hill, 1965], p. 357).

10. I remember from my grandfather's generation that there were clothes one wore during the week and clothes which were worn only on Sundays.

11. Gregory Stone, *Mass Leisure* (New York: The Free Press, 1958), p. 257.

12. At one time men had canes to support them when they were strolling and undoubtedly also as a male symbol. They have disappeared, when leisurely walking disappeared.

13. For the external signs of masculinity, see the article "The Horseless Cowboys" by John A. Popplestone in *Trans-Action* (May/June, 1966), p. 25. He gives a detailed analysis of the popularity of Western clothes and boots in the United States and its relevance to the need of men to use these clothes and boots to display their masculinity and toughness. The sex appeal is obvious according to Popplestone. I quote: "The erotic aspect of cowboyhood is prominent in the advertising world: a shirt is 'tailored to fit close,' blue jeans are praised for 'snug-fitting crotch and tight-fitting legs.'"

CHAPTER VI

1. Edwin T. Bowden, *The Dungeon of the Heart* (New York: Macmillan, 1961), p. 5.

2. This in spite of the symphony orchestras numbered in the hundreds, the well-equipped university theaters, the proliferating literary conferences, and all the manifold expressions of the "cultural explosion."

3. Thomas Wolfe, *Look Homeward, Angel* (New York: Scribner's, 1929), pp. 423–24.

4. *Newsweek*, March 21, 1966. One may, of course, wonder how much talking about sex young men ever have done with their parents. If novels and plays are any indication, the need to inform their sons about sex has often been a source of embarrassment for fathers, and sons have been unwilling to discuss, not their conquests, perhaps, but their affectionate regard for a young girl. The cliché of "puppy love," which parents regard with ridicule or, at best, fond superiority, has tended to lessen in the past two decades; parents take their children's sexual attachments rather more seriously. Often the parent (this may be more common between mothers and daughters than fathers and sons) appears to be even overly involved with his youngsters in what might be called the battle for success in the peer group, where so much of the young people's

sexual experience occurs. With the loosening of manners and the
weakening of some taboos, the middle-class adolescent is less
apt to cross the railroad tracks for his first ventures into sexual
activity—a situation which may, perhaps, have some relation
to the prevalence of early marriage.

5. Edgar Z. Friedenberg, *The Vanishing Adolescent* (New
York: Dell, 1962).

6. Aged nineteen, which seems to indicate a certain degree
of retardation, or at least deviation from the customary pattern
of progress through school.

7. Gregory Corso, "Life, Death and Dancing: A Buffalo
Shindig" (*Esquire,* July, 1965).

8. The urban adolescent, in contrast, may be overtly hostile
to the formal schooling offered him, and with few desirable
job prospects, little room for sports, little money for parties,
often seems to alternate between blank-eyed idleness and a
kind of violence equally indicative of boredom.

9. What is most surprising to me in the increasing popularity
of the psychedelic drugs is the obvious withdrawal from the
world—i.e., the refusal to come to terms with the here-and-now
situation.

10. Young males are not the only people who are turning to
the hallucinogens, incidentally. Presumably mature persons
insist that the experience derived from their consumption is
useful, indeed religious.

11. Drug-taking in itself is *passive.* One waits for the effect
to take place. There is *no* active participation. It is indeed
characteristic of the passivity of the male in our contemporary
culture that he seeks refuge in passive drug-taking.

12. Since many homosexuals do marry, it is incorrect to
impute homosexuality to a single man over thirty as a mere
matter of course. Male homosexuality may have increased during the past three or four decades, but that may be a phenomenon more evident among younger age groups; the single man
past thirty who does not wish to marry may be a relic of another style of life, but he is not necessarily homosexual. See
"Men Alone: The Male Homosexual and the Disintegration
of the Family," in Hendrik M. Ruitenbeek, ed., *The Problem
of Homosexuality in Modern Society* (New York: E. P. Dutton,
1963).

13. W. H. Whyte, Jr., *The Organization Man* (New York:
Doubleday Anchor Books, 1957); John R. Seeley *et. al., Crest-
wood Heights* (New York: Basic Books, 1956); John Keats,
The Crack in the Picture Window (Boston: Houghton Mifflin,
1957).

14. Blue-collar suburbs exist, too, one should remember, but these have not been studied very much. This writer continues to view with interest the scantiness of explorations of the life of lower-income groups at a time when American sociologists and social psychologists are increasingly aware of growing status differences and class groupings in the United States. C. Wright Mills surveyed the white-collar group; there are numerous studies of delinquent youth and even the poverty-stricken segments of society from which so large a portion of delinquents come. But comparatively little work has been done with the skilled and semiskilled worker who is an important beneficiary of the affluent society. What shape does the conflict of generations take among these people—so many of them "ethnics"? What kinds of emotional response develop out of the distinctive patterns of sexual behavior which the Kinsey report, say, shows to exist among the lower classes? The questions awaiting investigation are many, and until adequate inquiries have been made, much contemporary sociological interpretation, especially that which is available to the nonprofessional reader, will remain of very restricted significance, applying only to the middle class.

15. In terms of comfort and service, the standard may be less high; repairs are sufficiently costly so that the man of the house may be compelled to do more himself than he enjoys, and few suburban families are so well off that the women can employ a full-time servant.

16. Some go into psychotherapy, of course, but even a professional analyst may wonder whether psychotherapy alone can give a person the inner resources which an entire social system seems to counterbalance. The man secure in himself might have an unprofitably high level of sales resistance, for example, resistance to consumer services. Suppose he preferred durables, and then what would happen to the economy?

CHAPTER VII

1. See, for example, Bruno Bettelheim, "Growing Up Female" (*Harper's Magazine*, October, 1962); and Morton M. Hunt, *Her Infinite Variety: The American Woman as Lover, Mate and Rival* (New York: Harper and Row, 1962).

2. Bruno Bettelheim, "The Problem of Generations" (*Daedalus*, Winter, 1962).

3. Some concerned observers in the hundredth anniversary number of the *Nation* pointed out that many male adolescents seemed to be taking a similar nonaggressive way to insulate themselves from the pressures of the dominant adult world. These youths, like women playing the tradition role, did not

openly resist. They did not quarrel with their families; they did not show political or even sexual rebelliousness; they were neither violent nor particularly promiscuous; they merely took refuge in a private world of heightened sensitivity, and what they considered sharpened sensation and more refined responses to experience by taking pills, potions, and powders: tranquilizers, energizers, narcotic cough syrups, marijuana, hallucinogens, and the like. Thus, they convinced themselves that despite visibly conventional behavior, they were really resisting the powerful adult world.

4. Leon Salzman, " 'Latent' Homosexuality," in Judd Marmor, ed., *Sexual Inversion* (New York: Basic Books, 1965).

5. And guns have so many fanciers nowadays that the psychoanalyst is tempted to think many of their possessors, despite the collector's interest they claim in acquiring these objects of no conceivable use, are actually trying to assure themselves that they have not really been castrated; they just feel that they have.

6. Alfred Kinsey *et. al.*, *Sexual Behavior in the American Male* (Philadelphia: Saunders, 1948), p. 569.

7. It is even more amazing to note that so many women still often do not *realize* that their men have *failed*. Regardless of our current sophistication with sexual matters, many women (and for that matter many men) are still poorly informed about what adequate sexual performance constitutes.

8. Leland E. Glover, *The Impotent Male* (Derby, Conn.: Monarch Books, 1963), p. 16.

9. English and Pearson in *Emotional Problems of Living* (New York: Norton, 1945) define impotence as the inability to achieve or maintain an erection "long enough to effect entrance into the vagina and . . . at least a few coital movements before ejaculation." See also E. W. Hirsch, *The Power To Love* (New York: Garden City Publishing Company, 1938); M. Levine, *Psychotherapy in Medical Practice* (New York: Macmillan, 1943); Karl A. Menninger, *Man Against Himself* (New York: Harcourt, Brace, 1938).

10. Wilhelm Stekel, *Impotence in the Male* (New York: Liveright, 1927), Vol. I, p. 10.

11. Especially in young couples (in treatment) I have observed a distinct pattern of sometimes fierce competition. Now that young women hold responsible career jobs (and are not just secretaries) the competition has become much stronger.

12. Leland Glover, *op. cit.*, p. 15.

13. Sylvia Brody, *Passivity: A Study of Its Development and Expression in Boys* (New York: International Universities Press, 1964).

14. The army, the prison, and the hospital already speak of "processing" those who enter them; schools and colleges are beginning to use the same kind of phrases. Perhaps "processing: stage one" will soon replace "birth" in our vocabulary, and "death" be succeeded by "scrapping."

15. Yet in emergencies, some Americans have found it difficult to endure a situation in which they experienced defeat by an enemy who challenged their basic social premise. There have been persistent reports that, during the Korean conflict, American war prisoners broke down more easily than others under enemy pressure. I have often wondered what foreign military occupation would have done to the exaggerated notions of loyalty which many Americans hold.

16. Richard Hofstadter, *The Paranoid Style in American Politics, and Other Essays* (New York: Knopf, 1965).

17. Betty Friedan, *The Feminine Mystique* (New York: Norton, 1963), p. 273. The author also declares that men have become more hostile to women, and even to sex, at the very time when women, influenced by the percolation of psychoanalytic ideas through the society, tend to retire from the feminism of the 1920's, say, and to be socially passive and sexually responsive, concerned with love and motherhood rather than with social justice and the achievement of opportunities for professional activity and distinction.

18. See Thomas Szasz in Judd Marmor, ed., *op. cit.* Contrary to popular notions, the passive male is not necessarily homosexual, latently or overtly.

19. I want to clarify the term "distortion" here. I can see that in a predominantly heterosexual culture, as ours, homosexuality is to be considered a distortion from the cultural pattern. However, that does not imply a moral or clinical judgment. I hold with Freud that homosexuality is neither an illness nor a vice. Moreover, it does not even have to be neurotic.

20. Leon Salzman, in Judd Marmor, ed., *op. cit.*, pp. 235, 242.

21. Or look, for that matter, at the lower-class Irish subculture in New York, where men spend most of their free time in the bar drinking with other men.

22. In discussing dormant homosexuality, practical factors should not be ignored. Homosexual behavior is against the law in the United States (except for Illinois). Cultural pressures against homosexuality are thus reinforced. In Holland, where the law does not penalize homosexual behavior, psychotherapists report rather a low incidence of dormant homosexuality. Interestingly, there has been an increase in overt homosexuality

among the lower-income groups in The Netherlands.

   23. Judd Marmor, ed., *op. cit.*, pp. 250–51, 275.

CHAPTER VIII

   1. May one hazard a conjecture that a new status shift is taking place in contemporary culture? A number of observers have noted that, in England and the United States particularly, lower-class youth seem to be setting patterns of social style—clothes, entertainment, and haircuts. It may be argued that much of the influence of the new style is to be attributed to press agentry and advertising, for style can become fashion and fashion provides merchandise which can be sold. One wonders, nevertheless, whether such merchandising efforts could have succeeded without antecedent factors, notably money in the possession of lower-class youth—a situation especially evident and novel in England—and the presence of numbers of slightly older people, impatient of traditional cultural standards, who have more money than capacity to invent ways of amusing themselves. It is the shift of standards among the latter group which constitutes a status change.

   2. Richard Hofstadter, *The Age of Reform: From Bryan to F.D.R.* (New York: Knopf, 1955).

   3. Bruno Bettelheim in Erik H. Erikson, ed., *The Challenge of Youth* (New York: Doubleday Anchor Books, 1965), p. 101.

   4. Leslie Farber, "I'm Sorry, Dear" (*Commentary*, November, 1964), pp. 47–48, 54; also in Leslie Farber, *The Ways of the Will* (New York: Basic Books, 1966).

   5. The Masters study, which was originally undertaken to explore the physiological aspects of male impotence, was broadened to include a laboratory study and motion-picture recording of the female body under autostimulation. It has since been published by Little, Brown and Co. in Boston under the title *Human Sexual Response*.

   6. Edgar Z. Friedenberg in *The Vanishing Adolescent* (New York: Dell, 1962) and *Coming of Age in America* (New York: Random House, 1965), and Kenneth Keniston in *The Uncommitted* (New York: Harcourt, Brace and World, 1965) have pointed out the threat of alienation to the morals of contemporary young people.

CHAPTER IX

   1. The presentation of choice to the contemporary patient is often amazing. The thought of being able to make a choice and the availability of such a choice have never occurred to him. Still it is there for him to take and to exercise.

   2. Specific solutions are difficult to give, but fathers in the

family can express their sense of spontaneity and adventure in many ways. Do they still take their sons for a walk? Without becoming a buddy the father in today's family can find ways and means to get closer to his children. The emphasis should be on the sharing of their experiences.

Have you read these paperbacks from